Becoming
Becoming Yourself

MW01037863

Becoming a Leader Is Becoming Yourself

RUSS S. MOXLEY

McFarland & Company, Inc., Publishers

Jefferson, North Carolina

LIBRARY OF CONGRESS CATALOGUING-IN-PUBLICATION DATA

Moxley, Russ S., 1944–
    Becoming a leader is becoming yourself / Russ S. Moxley.
        p.   cm.
    Includes bibliographical references and index.

    ISBN 978-0-7864-9738-6 (softcover : acid free paper) ∞
    ISBN 978-1-4766-1877-7 (ebook)

    1. Leadership.   2. Industrial management.   3. Organizational
effectiveness.   I. Title.

    HD57.7.M687 2015
    658.4'092—dc23   2015014652

BRITISH LIBRARY CATALOGUING DATA ARE AVAILABLE

Front cover image © Ale-ks/Thinkstock

Printed in the United States of America

McFarland & Company, Inc., Publishers
    Box 611, Jefferson, North Carolina 28640
        www.mcfarlandpub.com

For my daughters and my wife:
Ashley, Lindsey, Laurie, Amy and Jean,
with gratitude and love for helping me
become the person I started out to be.

Contents

7

Preface and Acknowledgments

The Bedrock Idea

There is a single clear conviction that provides the bedrock for this book and it is captured in the title: *Becoming a Leader Is Becoming Yourself.* It is becoming a whole and authentic self.

I did not come to this conviction quickly or easily. I spent many years focused on the skills, competencies and knowledge leaders needed if they were to be effective. What are the tasks of leadership, I asked, and how are they different from the tasks of management? How can I and others most effectively accomplish these tasks? What are the competencies that are needed to create a bold and energizing vision, develop alignment with that vision, and produce lasting and useful change? What are mission statements and goals and strategies, and how can they best be defined and used? How can change be navigated and conflict orchestrated effectively? These were not only the questions I asked; they were the questions asked and answered in a plethora of books written, academic courses taught, and leadership development courses offered, including courses I taught. Effective leadership depended on knowing what to do and how to do it, or so I thought.

Other writers and leadership theorists have looked in other places for the key to leadership effectiveness. They looked at traits like charisma that they imagined individuals needed to graft onto their personality to be effective leaders. They examined the relationship between leader and follower. They developed contingency models of leadership. They wrote about "habits," "laws" or tips and techniques that promised success. They wrote articles and biographies of ideal leaders and encouraged aspiring leaders to emulate them.

For me, and for others, the assumption seems to have been that there is something "out there" that will insure leadership effectiveness. All individuals have to do is identify and then adopt this illusory "something," and they too could be a leader, or so we thought.

For the almost forty years that I have trained in leadership development programs, served as a coach to executive men and women, and have been a practicing leader in two different organizations, I have paid scant attention to the identity of the leader, either as it relates to myself or to the leaders with whom I have been privileged to work. The thought of doing so never occurred to me, not often, and never in a pressing way. I had a faint notion that things like wholeness and authenticity mattered, but mostly I focused on things like vision and goals, strategies and tactics, alignment and resource allocation. I thought effective leadership could be defined by the right competency models, and I worked hard to develop those models.

Slowly it dawned on me, as one experience built on another, that the "what" and "how" of leadership are important but not sufficient. I learned that individuals can be provided knowledge about leadership tasks, and all the right competencies, but unless they are willing to show up and state clearly their deep hopes for the future direction of the organization, nothing changes. I realized that individuals can be taught the skills and perspectives needed to appropriately speak their truth, confront others, and orchestrate conflict, but unless they have the courage to use those skills, and until they accept their accountability for outcomes, nothing will be different. I observed men and women trying to emulate someone they admired rather than being themselves, wearing one face and then another as they engaged in leadership tasks. I worked for leaders who adopted one technique or another, or tried some simple formula for leadership effectiveness, rather than become and be themselves. But none of that worked, not fully, not finally.

Leaders are trusted and their leadership is effective when they know who they are and when their leadership is rooted in their whole and authentic self. It is just that simple, and just that hard. It is hard because it takes time, energy, focus and courage to become and be our true self and engage in leadership from that exact spot, but we can muster the courage and lead from this place. It has been done, it is being done, and we can do it.

Wholeness and Authenticity

The promise and central premise of this book is that leadership effectiveness is rooted in the wholeness and authenticity of the person.

By authenticity I mean "real-ness." When I am being real there is no difference between my "game face" and my real face; I state my position on critical issues and do so without spinning the truth; I act on my core values even when the heat is on, and I do not say "yes" when I want to say "no." When I am being real I am "perfectly Russ"—a person with gifts and limits—not the idealized person I have spent way too much time and energy trying to convince myself and others was the real me. And when I am real, others trust me.

Wholeness is just as important as authenticity, but a bit harder to understand. Hang with me. My belief is that you and I were born whole—in the words of Franciscan priest Richard Rohr we were born "innocent." Then during the process of socialization one experience after another wounds us, and we begin to separate parts of ourselves—we separate inner life from outer work (we learn to hide some of the thoughts and feelings we cherish), we separate our public and private persona, and we separate our physical, mental, emotional and spiritual energies. Wholeness requires that we integrate or fuse these separated parts of ourselves into one. The journey to wholeness, to being restored, is how I understand the purpose of the leadership journey, the personal journey, and the spiritual journey.

These ideas will be explored in depth throughout the book; for now, I invite you to join me in a consideration of how these ideas impact your practice of leadership.

Weaving Threads

I like weaving. I am a synthesizer. I love to do what poet Rainer Maria Rilke suggested years ago: take ideas that seem like "ill-matched threads and weave them into a single cloth," and do so in novel and, I hope, helpful ways. I have done this in my vocation, in my experiences as a practicing manager/leader, and in the opportunities I have had to write.

In the first book I wrote, *Leadership and Spirit,* I wove the threads of leadership and spirit together. I linked spirit, the breath of life, to different ways of understanding and practicing leadership. I argued that some practices of leadership leave people feeling dispirited, while other practices were inspiriting. In this book the weaving continues but the focus is different. The shift is from practices of leadership to the journey each of us takes to become whole and authentic persons and leaders. On this journey there are many different threads of our self that we must weave to become a whole and integrated person.

We must weave the threads of *inner life and outer work.* Over time I have learned that what goes on in our inner life affects, for good and bad, our engagement in leadership. And conversely what goes on while we are leading affects our inner life. The inner life of the leader is not terrain usually covered in books and workshops and classes on leadership, but as I explain later, when we don't weave inner life and outer work we create havoc.

We must weave the threads of *mental, physical, emotional and spiritual energy.* Some American Indian tribes teach that we are each a house with four rooms, but often we do not see the thread that weaves between and among these rooms. Too often we think that we can take our physical and mental energy to work, but leave emotional and spiritual energy at home, or at least locked safely in the trunk of our car in the company parking lot. As you read on, you will learn why I believe that becoming who we are and effectively accomplishing leadership tasks requires the use of all of our energies.

We must weave our *gifts and limits,* our *strengths and weaknesses.* We each have gifts and skills to offer to the accomplishment of leadership tasks. It is important that we each discern, claim and use those gifts and skills. Only then can we make the contribution that is distinctively ours to make. At the same time we must acknowledge our limits and weaknesses. As I explain in detail later, there are things we cannot do, and ought not to try to do, as a leader. On our journeys we learn how to own our limits and work within them.

We must weave *light and shadow*. All of us cast light and shadow. We wish we didn't; we like the idea of casting light, but do not like thinking that we create dark places through which others must find their way and do their work. What makes the idea of casting shadow even more troublesome is that when we are working on leadership tasks, the shadow we cast is a longer one. One of the hardest parts of the journey to becoming a whole and authentic person is the journey down and in to identify and integrate our shadow. Weaving light and shadow is an on-going, lifelong process.

We must also weave the strands of *who we are as whole men and women—as individuals—with who we are as part of community*. Historically, in the United States we have thought of leadership as being the province of strong, even extraordinary, individuals. We expected these leaders to create a compelling vision, articulate it in an inspiring way, and help us navigate the whitewaters of change. To be sure, part of our development is to grow into an awareness of our true self, to discern and learn to use our gifts, and to accept responsibility for ourselves. This process is known as individuation. When we do not complete this process, we too easily lose a sense of ourselves, and we allow others to define us. We accommodate the needs of others too quickly.

As I wrote in my first book, there is a difference, though, between individuation and rugged individualism. We often confuse the two. We believe that completing the process of individuation means that we must always stand on our own two feet, be the one who creates a direction for our organization, makes the important strategic directions, be the heroic leader always leading the parade. Being part of a community—a great group like an executive team or a group of supervisors on the shop floor—and acting interdependently is seen as too soft. But I have learned I am most effective when I realize that I am part of a larger ecosystem. And I have learned when I offer my gifts and skills and energies to the accomplishment of leadership tasks, and other ordinary individuals do the same, outstanding results can be accomplished. Strong individuals are still important, but equally important is a community of individuals who are ready and willing to help accomplish the leadership tasks.

For years I have worked to weave together the threads of *leadership development, personal development and spiritual development*. These three threads are often seen as so different that "never the twain shall meet." Instead of attempting to weave them together, we attempt to keep them separate and distinct, each in its separate sphere. I have been trying to synthesize them for years. Today, I believe that, properly understood, *leadership development is personal development is spiritual development.* I invite you to think about this throughout the book, but especially in the postscript.

William Stafford is one of my favorite poets—and my eleventh grade English teacher would be astonished to hear that I love poetry—and I often reflect on "The Way It Is." Stafford writes, "There's a thread you follow" and "while you hold it you can't get lost." One of the threads I have been following for the past several years is attempting to see things whole—see myself and you as whole, see what seem to be "ill-fitting" threads as part of the whole cloth. One of my intentions in this book is to offer ways we can all see things whole.

Two Invitations

As you read and consider the ideas in this book I invite you to tap into your own deep knowledge about life and leadership. By reflecting on your experiences, I believe you will find that you have an inner wisdom about yourself and about leadership. Too often you and I allow ourselves to be held captive by empiricism, rationalism and scientism— by data that exists "out there." While data is important and these "isms" have served us well in so many areas of life, these days we tend to believe something is true only if there is empirical and verifiable data to support it. But beyond the rational and scientific, beyond the empirical data, there is another level of knowing.

One way we get in touch with this different level of knowing is to slow down, honor silence, listen to our own inner wisdom, and pay attention to what emerges from our depths. So, as you read this book and pay attention to the stories I share, please also pay attention to truths—including transrational truths—that go beyond the data.

The second invitation is to think about how the ideas about life and leadership apply to you. If you are like me, you often think about the "leaders" you know when reading a book on leadership. Instead of thinking about "them" and what they do I encourage you to think about yourself and where you are on the journey to becoming yourself and an authentic leader.

The Audience

For whom is this book written? This is always an interesting question for me. My first response is that it is written for me. I grew up thinking that when I understood something well enough I might write about it. Now I know it is in the process of writing itself that I begin to understand. It is only when I am nearing the end of the process that I begin to consider for whom else it might be written.

Through the years I have been privileged to work with leaders from many different sectors—business leaders, nonprofit leaders, public sector leaders, religious leaders, and civic leaders. I have learned from them and with them. As I wrote this book, I often told myself I needed to pick one of these audiences and write for them, that it would not work to write for all of them. But I resisted the idea that I needed to write to only one audience of leaders; it would not be seeing things whole. And, though I do not want to minimize the differences, I have learned over time that men and women from these different sectors are more alike than different, the leadership challenges they face are more similar than dissimilar, and that all must take the journey to becoming their true and authentic selves. This book is written for those men and women from every sector who yearn to be authentic and to practice leadership in a different and more effective way. It is written for those who long to weave the threads of their lives, to experience themselves as whole and integrated, to be real people in life and at work.

The book is also written for those who do not now think of themselves as leaders. My belief, shaped by years of experience, is that at some point in our lives all of us will have the opportunity to be engaged in leadership tasks. The central message in the prologue says it simply: leadership is everyone's vocation (and this phrase is in a longer quote from Parker J. Palmer). We may engage in this vocation in our family, in our neighborhood, in our church, mosque or synagogue, in a civic organization or political party, or in the places we work. It is no longer useful for us to think of leadership as something that "they" provide; today, we need to understand leadership as something "we" offer.

The Structure of the Book

There are three interrelated sections to this book. The first section is the first chapter, a chapter in which I make the case that "leadership is everyone's vocation." This chapter provides an important context for the second section, five chapters in which the focus is on the journey that each of us—everyone—must take to become and be whole and authentic persons and leaders. The final section begins with chapter seven and includes three chapters that extend and expand the ideas offered in the first two sections. The final chapter is a postscript in which I weave together leader development, personal development and spiritual development.

Acknowledgments

As you read on you will learn that I believe that effective leadership often emerges from high-quality interactions between and among people. So it is with this book. This book was not created by me alone; it emerged from the relationships I have had with many friends and teachers, colleagues and clients. There were times as I was writing when ideas were flowing and it seemed to me that I was simply a channel for them; the ideas themselves emerged from relationships. If I deserve credit for anything, it is for linking the ideas in novel and useful ways. I hope I have done this. At the risk of leaving some out, I want to acknowledge some of my "teachers" who have been especially important to me.

The Center for Creative Leadership (CCL), a nonprofit educational and research organization headquartered in Greensboro, North Carolina, provides me the opportunity to do what is right work for me— leadership development work—with good colleagues and with leaders from a wide variety of organizations. I consider the time I have worked with CCL a thirty-year leadership development experience; I have grown as a person and grown in my understanding of leadership. Even the experiences that CCL researchers have labeled "hardships" have been developmental. I have also developed clear and helpful insights about *leader development*—the various ways that I and other individuals acquire the skills and perspectives needed to be effective in leadership roles. To my colleagues at CCL, and to the clients who taught me as I was attempting to teach them, my deep thanks.

During the time I was at CCL, I began co-designing and co-facilitating the Reynolds Program in Church Leadership, a year-long program for United Methodist Ministers from four states, offered in and by CCL and the United Methodist Foundation of Western North Carolina. The program is, for me, leadership development done right. The focus of the program parallels the theme of this book: the point is not to become a leader; the point is to become our self and be our self as we engage in leadership tasks. As I have facilitated workshops for hundreds of clergy leaders I have also learned and grown and changed. I have developed new and deeper understandings of leadership, have become more aware of how leaders from different sectors are more similar than dissimilar, and have sharpened my belief that there are new and better ways to do leadership.

Over the past twelve years I have been deeply involved in the work offered in and through the Center for Courage and Renewal (CCR), an organization founded by Parker J. Palmer. The work I do in association with CCR encourages me to become and be myself—my whole and authentic self—and has provided me with a deeper awareness of the courage required to do so. There are many life forces that bend me—and I suspect you—out of shape, but the people who have been colleagues and fellow sojourners in my work with CCR are helping me uncover my original shape. To all those who are part of the CCR network or with whom I have been privileged to sit in a "circle of trust," I offer my profound gratitude.

Several people read various version of this book and each gave caring and helpful counsel to me. Dianne Rawlins and Nathan Kirkpatrick read earlier versions and gave me helpful feedback and encouragement to keep writing. Jane Beatty, a friend and gifted wordsmith and grammarian, and Megan Scribner, an editor extraordinaire, read a later version, offered keen insights, asked penetrating questions and suggested important revisions. The book is better because of their contributions.

It takes a village to raise a child; it takes friends like these to write a book like this.

Finally, I am surrounded by what one of my daughters used to call "love people"—family members—who have been trustworthy traveling companions on my journey. To my wife, my daughters, my stepdaughters, my grandchildren, my sons-in-law, and my sisters and their families, my heartfelt thanks and my love.

PART ONE:
SETTING THE CONTEXT

1. Leadership Is Everyone's Vocation

The first essential message of this book is that "leadership is everyone's vocation."

We do not usually think of leadership in this way. In most organizations "they" are the leaders; "we" are the followers. From the time of the Great Man theory until today, we have assumed that "they" have extraordinary traits or abilities that "we" mere mortals do not have. And because "they" have attributes that set them apart, we think that "they" are responsible for accomplishing leadership tasks—crafting and articulating a compelling vision, building alignment with that vision, and successfully steering the organizational craft through the whitewater of change necessary to accomplish the vision. And they are, of course, the men and women at the top of the organization. This understanding of leaders and leadership has been the dominant narrative for years. I call it the executive-as-leader practice of leadership. In this view leadership is the vocation of a select few men and women, not of everyone.

To be fair to the "they," many of us who are the "we" like it this way. It gets us off the hook. If "they" are responsible and accountable, "we" are not. When there is not a clear direction for the organization, when there is no real commitment to a strategic plan, when the craft is getting tossed to and fro in the whitewater, it is the leader's fault, not ours. Harvard professor Ron Heifitz makes the same point this way, "those who consider themselves 'not leaders' escape responsibility for taking action, or for learning how to take action, when they see a need. In face of critical problems they [the "we"] say, 'I am not a leader, what can I do'"? (1994, p. 20). As long as you and I trade our freedom for some shaky promise of security, "they" will be seen as "the leaders." Until you and I accept that we are accountable for the outcomes, the executive-as-leader model will continue to dominate.

When we think of leaders as having extraordinary capacities, as having traits or attributes that elevate them, we put them on a pedestal and expect higher levels of insight and behavior from them. We do not want to think that our leaders have gifts and limits, that they cast light and shadow, or that they have feet of clay. Instead we want ideal leaders, and we project our notion of ideal onto them. Then, when these leaders disappoint us, as they almost always do, we do not consider that we are operating with an unrealistic understanding of leadership. Instead, we look at each other with a sigh and say, "we have the wrong leader." There is something wrong with the person, we think, not with our mental model.

This does not always happen, of course. There are individuals at the top of some organizations who are authentic and whole, who keep their egos in check, who are not seduced by the trappings of their position, and who lead with a deep sense of integrity. One name given to these men and women are servant leaders. Several years ago I got to know the president of a large heating and air conditioning company. He told me stories of how leadership tasks were accomplished collaboratively in his organization (in the words of Peter Block he saw himself as a host, not a hero), and shared other stories of how he understood his role as serving the needs of the company and its employees. He was a man of strong opinion and high expectations who did not abdicate his responsibility to make sure leadership happened in the company, but he felt no need to do it all alone, no need to be "the leader."

Another name given to these individuals is "Level 5 leaders," a phrase coined by Jim Collins and used in his book, *Good to Great*. Collins wrote, "Level 5 leaders display a compelling modesty, are self-effacing, and understated. In contrast, "two-thirds of the comparison companies had leaders with gargantuan personal egos that contributed to the demise of continued mediocrity of the company" (2001, p. 39).

Even with these notable exceptions, many individuals and organizations cling to the old mental models and to the belief there are great men (and women) who are extraordinary and who will keep us safe and secure. This understanding of leadership is tired, worn thin if not worn out. It no longer serves us well. It is not helpful in today's post-industrial world. There are several reasons this is so:

- *The changing nature of work and workers makes the traditional paradigm or mental model less viable.* In the industrial era, Frederick Taylor told employers they needed workers who had "brawn, not brains," but today a primary source of competitive advantage is intellectual capital, and to succeed organizations need knowledge workers. These knowledge workers are spread throughout the organization, not clustered at the top. This fact alone makes the executive-as-leaders practice of leadership less viable. Noted author Warren Bennis says something similar, "To a large degree our growing recognition of the need for a new, more collaborative form of leadership results from the emergence of intellectual capital as the most important element of organizational success" (1997, p. 84).
- *The increasing diversity of the workforce makes the traditional paradigm less possible.* It was not that long ago that the workforce was more homogeneous, and workers were more similar than dissimilar in their backgrounds and values. In those days it was more likely that a leader could create a vision that represented the hopes and aspirations of all followers. But today, when the demographics of the workforce have changed and are changing, it is far less likely that one person, no matter how far-sighted, can create a bold and compelling vision that will be shared by all.
- *Individual leaders cannot, by themselves, meet the adaptive challenges their organizations face.* Individual leaders are quite capable of solving most of the technical challenges their organizations face; they have the skills and experience necessary to do so. By definition, technical challenges are those where there is a right answer and this answer can be known by the executive-as-leader. But as Ron Heifitz has so clearly pointed out, today's organizations are facing a different kind of challenge—adaptive, not technical—and these challenges are new and different. There is no one right answer to these adaptive challenges. Leaders do not have the skills or

requisite experience needed to address them by themselves. A new practice of leadership—a practice that engages the skills and experience of many different people—is needed to accomplish adaptive work.

John Ryan, current president of the Center for Creative Leadership, made a similar point in a recent newspaper article about CCL. He said, "We focus more on making sure that the days of superman are over. We have a VUCA world: volatility, uncertainty, complexity, ambiguity … you'd better develop a great executive team because you are only going to handle this complexity if you get the best from everybody" (Barron 2011, B1–2).

The phrase, "leadership is everyone's vocation," with which this chapter started, is a phrase from a longer quote from Parker J. Palmer. Palmer writes, "Leadership is a concept we often dismiss. It seems immodest, even self-aggrandizing, to think of ourselves as leaders. But if it is true that we are made for community, then leadership is everyone's vocation, and it can be an invasion to insist it is not. When we live in an ecosystem called community, everyone follows and everyone leads" (2000, page 74). Everyone follows and everyone leads. No more "they" and "we." No more artificial distinctions between leaders and followers. The new mental model is based on the assumption that each of us has important gifts and skills to offer the crafting of vision and the setting of direction, to maintaining alignment and commitment, and to modeling the core values of the organization.

Understanding leadership as everyone's vocation is the new narrative that is needed to meet the challenges of today's world and best serve the purposes of today's organizations. Today we need a practice of leadership that is less hierarchical, more trust-based, and more interactive. Today we need an understanding and practice of leadership that does not rely solely on the extraordinary gifts of a single individual, but instead honors and uses the gifts and skills and energies of many ordinary individuals. Today individual genius still matters but not more than the creative collaboration of many bright, talented and diverse men and women.

Today a different way of thinking about and practicing leadership is emerging. Over the years we have defined leadership in many different ways, and have developed many different criteria for what constitutes effective leadership. Out of one of the first studies of leadership came what is known as the "great man" theory of leadership—leaders were extraversion-oriented, had above average intelligence, and had a tendency toward dominance. Then we studied traits like charisma because we though they would help us identify effective leaders. Later we developed contingency models of leadership and began to think leadership effectiveness could only be understood in relationship to a particular situation or context. More recently theorists and practitioners alike have argued that effective leadership can best be understood by examining the relationship between leaders and followers; in the recent past many organizations have been attracted to, and adopted, some version of servant leadership (while others have argued that the very name, servant leadership, is an oxymoron). Added to all this, we have had as many different definitions of leadership as we have people writing about it.

A different way to think about or conceptualize leadership is in terms of the tasks that must be accomplished, the work that must be done, for people in any organization or community to believe they have effective leadership. As I have studied the literature on leadership, observed and worked with leaders from many different backgrounds over the years, and especially as I have learned from research colleagues at the Center for Creative Leadership, I have come to believe that there are three essential tasks of leadership:

- Creating and articulating a compelling vision or sense of direction
- Developing alignment with that vision (making sure people and systems and structures are in alignment)
- Maintaining commitment to the vision

Over and over again, in one organization or another, I have found when these tasks are accomplished the men and women of the organization will say they have good leadership. But absent any one of these and people will bemoan the fact that their organization lacks leadership. These tasks can be accomplished by those who have charisma and those who do not, by those who use certain habits and those who choose not to, by those who are out front and leading the parade and those who remain in the background. The point is that is the accomplishment of these tasks—not traits or personality types or the use of certain formulas—that define leadership effectiveness.

When these leadership tasks are effectively accomplished the end result will be lasting and useful change. Several years ago John Kotter, then a professor at Harvard, argued that this end goal of producing lasting and useful change is what distinguishes leadership from management. Producing change, Kotter wrote, "is the primary function of leadership" (1990, p. 7). The primary reason any organization or group of people takes the time and spends the energy necessary to create a new vision or new sense of direction, develop alignment with it, and maintain commitment to it, is to bring about change or renewal.

The way we think about leadership is changing; the way we practice leadership is also changing. Certainly, this different way of practicing leadership is not all that new. For years we have talked about distributed leadership or relational leadership or leadership-as-partnership. What's new is the growing realization of just how much this new practice of leadership is needed in the new times in which we live.

The fundamental difference in this new practice and the one with which we have lived and worked is that the source of leadership is different. In our traditional understanding leadership comes from within a person—and it is usually the extraordinary person at the top of the organization who is responsible for accomplishing the leadership tasks. In the emerging practice the source of leadership comes from relationship. It emerges from the quality of interaction between two or more people; it comes out of the give and take of relationships in which each person is acting with a deep sense of integrity. The leadership tasks are accomplished by a collective—a pair, a great group, a division of a larger organization, an entire company or community group. In this different practice of leadership there is no more "them" and "us"; now it is "we." The variations on this theme are as many and varied as the practice of leadership is implemented, but the result is the same—we are individually and collectively responsible for crafting a vision or setting a direction, for developing alignment with it, and for maintaining commitment to it.

In leadership-as-partnership the individual is still important. The difference is that now all individuals are important. There is no more than or less than, no one up or one down. One assumption beneath this new practice is that all individuals have important contributions to make to the accomplishment of the leadership tasks; a second is that they will make their contribution given the right opportunity and encouragement.

The contributions that each person has to make will be different, of course, and this is exactly what makes partnerships so viable. One person will be better able to imagine future possibilities, while another is more gifted at putting "arms and legs" on the vision. The energies of one individual can be best used to develop alignment with the vision, while another is more skilled at navigating the whitewater of change. The key point is that each of us has gifts and skills and energies to offer to the accomplishment of leadership tasks.

A look at the writing of Warren Bennis and his colleagues shows how the narrative about leaders and leadership has evolved and is evolving. A few years after writing *Leaders* with Bert Nanus, a book about executives-as-leaders, Bennis coauthored *Co-Leaders* with David A. Heenan. In the first chapter of this book Bennis and Heenan argue that we will never understand the genius that is Microsoft unless we understand the partnership that existed between Bill Gates and Steve Ballmer. Leadership emerged from their relationship, from the quality of their interaction. "Co-leadership is a tough-minded strategy that will unleash the hidden talent in any enterprise ... it celebrates those who do the real work, not just the few charismatic, often isolated leaders" (1999, jacket cover). There were eleven other stories in *Co-Leaders*, stories that illustrate that leadership is sometimes the province of a pair, not a person.

After *Co-Leaders,* Bennis teamed with Patricia Ward Biederman to write *Organizing Genius: The Secrets of Creative Collaboration.* In this important work Bennis and Biederman describe how leadership evolves from the interaction between and among people in "great groups." They told the story of seven: Apple Computer, the Black Mountain Artistic Community, President Clinton's Re-election Campaign Committee, Walt Disney's animation studio, the well-known "skunkworks" of Lockheed, the Manhattan Project, and Xerox's Palo Alto Research Center. After studying how leadership emerges from relationships among people working together, Bennis and Biederman concluded, "In a global society, in which timely information is the most desirable commodity, collaboration is not simply desirable, it is inevitable. In all but the rarest of cases, one is too small a number to produce greatness" (1997, p. 3). It is critical, at least at times, to see leadership as the province of a group, not a person.

Many executives-as-leaders, though, don't like groups. Instead, they demean them. "A camel is a horse designed by a committee," they jest. Too slow and inefficient, they complain. To be sure, some groups are inefficient and ineffective; but then again, so are some individual leaders. But when groups work well—when the gifts and skills and energies of all are honored and used—creative and bold leadership results.

When a group is responsible for accomplishing leadership tasks the process will likely be messier or more chaotic, there will be push and pull between and among group members, some tension will be inevitable, and it may take longer, but the direction that emerges will have richness and texture to it and be much more likely to represent the deep longings and preferred future of all the various stakeholders. There must still be alignment with the vision, but now alignment happens not because an individual leader is inspiring and energizing, but because individuals tend to support what they help create.

Leadership tasks can also be accomplished by entire organizations. In an earlier book, *Leadership and Spirit* (1999), I wrote about the practice of leadership at Southwest Airlines. The stories about this airline are stories from which legends are made, but one quote is particularly relevant and instructive: "Leadership is practiced through collaborative relationships. The people of Southwest Airlines work in relationships where the role of leader and employee are interchangeable" (1996, p. 299).

The story of Southwest Airlines is but one of many stories of organizations who are evolving new and different ways of accomplishing leadership tasks. In fits and starts, with small successes and some difficulties, organizations from every sector are learning that leadership is everyone's vocation, and that they—the organizations—are better when it is so.

Leadership and Management: A Quick Side Trip

It might be helpful to remember that we are talking about leadership tasks, not management functions, being accomplished through a collaborative process. Through the years there have been good and helpful arguments about whether there are essential differences between leadership and management. The two are inextricably linked and all organizations need both effective leadership and effective management, but there are differences. For example, if a leadership task is about setting direction, the related management task is to plan goals and objectives that will move the organization in the desired direction.

The reason for this quick side trip is that one objection often raised to the idea of leadership being the province of a pair or a group is that it would take too much time, if not be literally impossible, for a team to make *all* the decisions necessary to move an organization forward. My first response to this assertion: true enough. While some organizations are finding creative ways to have teams be responsible for accomplishing leadership tasks and management functions, my argument is that at least leadership tasks can be accomplished in a collective. Increasingly, and across a broad array of organizations, they are being accomplished in exactly this way.

My second response to the assertion that collective leadership takes too much time is that in the traditional paradigm it may take the executive-as-leader less time on the front end to create a vision but it often takes more on the back end to get alignment with that vision. The opposite is true for shared leadership: it may take more time to develop a shared sense of direction, but as suggested earlier, alignment is a natural by-product. One "large steeple" pastor I know wrote that it took him several years of seeding a vision in his church before it began to take root and grow. In contrast, I have worked with and in organizations where it took months of give and take to create a shared sense of direction, but no time to build alignment—it came with the process.

What the Skeptics Say

There are many executives-as-leaders, and just as many followers, who are not ready to let go of the traditional paradigm. In addition to the argument that any form of partnership would take too much time, the most pressing arguments of the skeptics, at least the ones I have heard, are three-fold.

The first line of defense is that the leadership-as-partnership diminishes the importance of the individual. We Americans hold tenaciously to our belief that it is the contribution of a single person that makes all the difference. One example of this is that time after time as I am describing the emerging paradigm I am encouraged to look again at the contribution Jack Welch made during his tenure as chairman and CEO of General Electric. By any measure of success, Welch's tenure was hugely successful. I do not and would not minimize the contribution Welch made to the accomplishment of leadership tasks at GE. But why is it, I wonder, that we so easily and readily focus on the singular contribution of one person like Jack Welch and ignore the contribution that literally thousands of dedicated men and women made as they showed up to work at GE each day?

Instead of diminishing the importance of outstanding individual leaders, what leadership-as-partnership offers is a way of elevating the role of the legion of employees of General Electric who use their gifts and skills to help set direction and find the way through adaptive challenges. Jack Welch clearly had gifts to offer to the company; the good news for GE and other companies is that others have gifts that differ and that complement those of the senior executives. When the gifts of all employees are acknowledged and used any company or community will be stronger and better.

Another argument against partnerships is that it is an individual, not a pair or a group, who must finally be accountable. If all are accountable, the argument goes, no one is accountable. The buck, we have always thought, must stop at a particular person's desk. This belief has a first cousin: accountability and authority must always be linked. In the industrial era this is how hierarchies worked, at least in theory: authority corresponded to management level in the organization, with the buck finally stopping at the CEO's door. It was argued that a supervisor or manager could not be held accountable unless he or she had authority, and this authority usually accompanied the position. The problem with this system is apparent: if accountability belongs only to those in positions of authority, "they" are responsible and "we" are not. It is another way that "we" get off the hook.

Partnerships require that all men and women of the company or community be responsible and accountable—to be accountable not

28

because we have been granted authority by someone else, but because we are the author of our own lives. In *Stewardship*, Peter Block says, "Each person is responsible for the outcomes and the current situation. There is no one else to blame. Partners have emotional responsibility for their own present and their own future ... the outcomes and quality of cooperation within a unit is everyone's responsibility"(1993, p. 30).

Let me be absolutely clear. Accountability is critical in any understanding and practice of leadership. And this accountability must be accepted by all partners engaged in accomplishing leadership tasks, whether the partnership is a pair, a team, or a larger collective. No ifs, ands, or buts; no finger-pointing and blaming others. When I have a place at the table, I must show up, be clear about my position, and accept responsibility for the outcome.

The third argument against shared leadership is that it simply will not work in times of crises, when there is an emergency, when risks run high. In times of crises we long for and think we need a traditional leader—a hero of sorts—who will save us from peril. An insurance executive voiced this opinion rather strongly in a group discussion I was leading, when he said, "in crises I want to work for a strong, command-and-control leader who, if he says, 'march over the edge of the ship,' everyone marches over the edge." Peter Block calls this the "romanticizing of leadership ... this love of leaders limits our capacity to create an alternative future" (2008, p. 41). Instead of romanticizing leaders, what is needed is an understanding that the greater the risk, the more adaptive the challenge, the more the "gifts, skills and energies" of all people is needed. Well-known author Meg Wheatley agrees, "Reflective leaders, including those in the military, have learned the higher the risk the more we need everyone's commitment and intelligence" (2005, p. 65).

Foundation Stones for Leadership-as-Partnership

For those ready to accept leadership as part and parcel of their vocation, there are particular perspectives that are important and practices that will help.

- *See through a new lens.* We need to be aware of our mental models, and the way those models blind us to new possibilities. Because of our mental models, we do not notice the leadership tasks being accomplished by a pair or group. The lens we look through enables us to see an activity as leadership only when it is being exercised by a bold, out-front individual. This reality was brought home to me several years ago when a prominent citizen in my city complained to me about our mayor because of the mayor's lack of leadership. When I asked what he meant, he was quite specific: the mayor was not bold enough, not willing to take strong stands on the issues, he waited to see which way the parade was going and then got out front. In truth, this was a mayor who worked behind the scenes to bring diverse groups together, who let a sense of direction emerge from discussions, and then who took the plan to city council for their consideration. Perhaps the mayor was not a leader in the traditional sense, but leadership tasks were getting accomplished, and thus, from my perspective, leadership was happening. This mayor was adding her chapter to a new narrative.
- *Suspend judgments.* The belief in "heroic" individual leaders is so deeply rooted into the fabric of our culture and companies that the first response to a different understanding and practice of leadership is that it simply will not work. I hear things like, "It will never work in our company"; "our senior management would not allow it"; "our people don't want it"; "you are too idealistic." Suspending judgment does not mean ignoring or denying these responses. It means, instead, noticing them and holding our assumptions in front of us— which means witnessing our thoughts and feelings without quickly acting on them. We will not engage in new practices of leadership until and unless we suspend judgments.
- *Notice opportunities.* Sometimes we do not engage in new ways of practicing leadership because we are not alert to opportunities. We are not always aware of the fact that we are charting a direction and that we need alignment. We separate the "planners" from the "implementers," and we limit

participation in the accomplishment of the leadership task of setting direction to the "planners." The terms "planners" and "implementers" comes from an exercise used in leadership development programs, an exercise that demonstrates in clear and concrete ways how easy it is to fall into the trap of thinking that there are leaders and followers. It demonstrates how often we assume that the role of the leader is to provide direction to the followers.

- *Pick partners wisely.* Not all pairs, teams, or groups can effectively accomplish leadership tasks. Not all collectives are "great groups." But processes of shared leadership are becoming increasingly important, and with it there is an increasing awareness of the importance of who is part of the collective. In *Good to Great*, Jim Collins writes about the importance of getting the wrong people off the bus and the right people on it. Diana Chapman Walsh, immediate past president of Wellesley College said a similar thing this way, "even if we know ourselves, we can't know all we need to know from our own limited perspective. And so we need to establish partnerships as the basic units for accomplishing work. And they have to be reliable partnerships, which means investing time and energy in preserving their integrity ... trustworthy leaders choose their partners wisely, for a range of perspectives and for a sense of shared core values ... enlisting others—and not just loyal insiders—in these mutual relationships becomes a major part of the leader's tasks" (2006, p. 22).
- *Practice new behaviors.* In recent years I was privileged to serve on the founding board of a small but growing international organization. We consciously worked at being a different kind of board and to practice a different kind of leadership, one characterized by working hard to forge a version of shared leadership. Each board member was committed to showing up, to being fully present, and to engaging in leadership tasks. We sat in a circle at our meetings, we left space in the circle for silence, we surfaced assumptions, we held differences without rushing to resolve

them, and we allowed decisions to emerge from the give and take of the conversation. Direction for the organization was co-created and alignment resulted from the way we worked together. This was a new way of being on a board for me. Sometimes I got impatient with the process and wanted to hurry things along—let's just vote and move on, I'd say to myself. But I learned, and we learned, to do leadership differently. We slowly found our way. And the leadership process, while new and different and sometimes difficult, was energizing.

- *Have patience.* It takes time for new understandings and practices of leadership to take hold. Habits and practices get embedded in organizations, and in the lives of individuals, and they are hard to break. All organizations, even the neighborhood book club to which my wife and I belong, have cultures—"ways we do things around here"—and often "the way we do things" includes the informal norms that have developed about how leadership happens. Changing "the way we do things around here" is hard work. So what to do? Look for windows of opportunities to practice leadership in a different way, a collective way. Celebrate small successes. Tell stories about those successes; it is the stories that get told that will re-culture a group or organization.

- *Don't wait for change to start at the top.* One of the illusions we cling to is that all change, including a change in the way leadership is understood and practiced, must start at the top. It is an excuse—a popular excuse today—for us not to change because "they" haven't or "they" won't let us. But I know of neighborhood groups in local communities who created momentum for change in the direction of their city, of task force groups in a business that developed and successfully promoted a new strategic thrust for the company, of a team of teachers who, by example and conscious effort, created a new vision for what was possible in a low-income neighborhood school. These groups and individuals remind us that we are each responsible and accountable, even when we are not in positions of formal authority. There are windows of opportunity throughout a community or a company for change to be initiated. When we understand that the phrase "leadership is everyone's vocation" applies to us, we will claim our personal power and initiate it on our own.

- *Share power.* Shared leadership or partnership cannot work when one person is powerful and others are not, or when one person chooses to use coercive power to force others to do something that they do not want to do. Instead, the emerging paradigm requires that all individuals claim their personal power—power based on self-confidence, competence, and character—and that they use their personal power for the benefit of the whole. "If we can practice our leadership within supportive communities—if we can build and bind those communities," Diana Chapman Walsh writes, "then we can begin to define and experience leadership as a collective project that derives its power and authority from a cooperative attachment to mutually defined commitments and values" (p. 24).

Because power is such an important dynamic in leadership, and because authoring our lives and claiming our power is one of the central tasks in our journey to becoming a whole and authentic person, we will focus our attention on it in a later chapter.

A Brief Summary

Today, leadership is everyone's vocation.

Today, the leader does not have to be all and do all; now we are all leaders.

There is a particular practice and process that can be used—I call it partnership—to accomplish leadership tasks, a practice that offers all people an opportunity to use their gifts and skills and energies.

This brings us to the close of this chapter and to a second essential message of this book. As suggested in the title, it is the bedrock conviction presented here: *becoming a leader is becoming yourself.*

PART TWO:
THE JOURNEY
TO AUTHENTIC LEADERSHIP

2. Becoming a Leader
Is Becoming Yourself

Author and well-known leadership theorist Warren Bennis gets right to the point: "The point is not to become a leader. The point is to become yourself, and to use yourself completely—all your gifts and skills and energies—to make your vision manifest. You must withhold nothing. You must, in sum, become the person you started out to be, and enjoy the process of becoming" (1989, pp. 111–112). Effective leadership is rooted in and emerges from the wholeness and authenticity of the person. It sounds so simple but is so hard: the point is not to become a leader; the point is to become yourself. Become the person you started out to be. Use yourself completely.

For many years, I and many others other missed the point. We invested precious resources—time, energy, and money—to help individuals become effective leaders, not become themselves. Through books, training programs, advanced degree programs, and in-house development efforts, we worked hard to help individuals develop the leadership competencies they needed. Our belief was that individuals both could and must develop the skills and perspectives needed to become leaders. We thought this was the point.

We also thought that if we provided the right tips and techniques, designed the right skill development experiences, taught the latest formula or theory du jour, helped graft a trait like charisma onto particular personality types, offered the latest biography and encouraged the emulation of an outstanding leader, or provided coaching on how to more effectively play a role, we would develop more effective leaders. Once again, we missed the point.

All these efforts were well-intended and most were important; most had something to offer in the development of the person and the leader, but our focus was wrong. We were developing leaders, not helping individuals become and be the person they started out to be.

What I have learned along the way is that individuals can learn different tips and techniques, new leadership theories, simple formulas for success, even develop the right competencies, and still never show up as a real person. This will not get us where we want to be, where others yearn for us to be, or where today's organizations need us to be.

Four beliefs provide the foundation for this chapter and this book:

First, we are always more or less our self. In the quote used at the start of the chapter Bennis focused on becoming—on our becoming the person we started out to be. But we are also and always being. We look retrospectively at a meeting of consequence in which we participated and say, "In that meeting I was myself—my whole self, my authentic self. I showed up." At other times we look back and realize we held our self at an arms-length distance, and instead of being our self we were the person others expected us to be. Our hope is that on the journey we can be our self more and more of the time.

Second, becoming our self is part, perhaps the most important part, of, a journey that continues throughout our lifetime. Many of us spend the first part, even the first half, of our lives trying to be the person others expect us to be. We play a role. We wear our game face to work. We emulate those we admire. Then, hopefully, at some point we turn toward home, toward becoming the person we started out to be. This process of becoming whole and authentic is the work of a life and a career. There are no short cuts, no buttons to push or levers to pull to speed up the process, no way to overnight wholeness and authenticity.

Third, organizations of every kind, and the people who work in them, yearn for whole and authentic leaders. We have tried other options and found them wanting. "Leadership requires the expression of an authentic self," wrote Rob Goffee and Gareth Jones. "Try to be like someone else—says Jack Welch, or Richard Branson or Michael Dell—and you will fail … our growing dissatisfaction with sleek, ersatz, airbrushed leadership is what makes authenticity such a desirable quality in today's corporations—a quality that, unfortunately, is in short supply" (2005, pp. 1, 3).

Finally, as we become our self—our whole and authentic self—we will also become more trustworthy and effective leaders. This is the point.

Becoming and being yourself (in this book I use true self and whole and authentic self interchangeably)—the person you started out to be—is a hard, tough journey. It is a journey that is full of speed bumps, detours, even some dead-ends. It is one that takes enormous courage to pursue. But it is a journey worth taking because it enables us to understand who we are at our core, allows us to engage in leadership wholly and fully, and takes us beyond ourselves so that we can be agents of change and transformation in our organizations and communities.

Being Someone Other Than Yourself

This central idea—that becoming a leader is becoming yourself—sounds simple, even simplistic—to many of the men and women with whom I have shared this notion in workshops and presentations. I often get the proverbial "well, duh" response. One executive even asked, "Who else could I be?" There are at least four answers to his question:

We can be a false self rather than a true self. To paraphrase a line from poet May Sarton's "Now I Become Myself," we often show up in life and leadership wearing someone else's face. We construct one false self and then another, one social personality or another, because we think we must if we are to be effective in our leadership roles and activities. We play a role rather than becoming and being ourselves. We do this, in part, because we want to be the person and leader others expect us to be. We also do it because we are not sure that the person we are is sufficient to accomplish leadership tasks. We do it because hiding behind one mask and then another seems safer and more secure. To be sure, there may be something of ourselves in each of these selves we construct, but none of them is our authentic self.

I am clear about the false self I tried hard to construct and present to others—it was my *idealized self.* The late Eric Berne, founder of Transactional Analysis that was popularized in the book, *I'm Okay, You're Okay,* said that one of the injunctions children pick up is to "be perfect." This is a message that drives many individuals for much of their lives.

For sure, it has driven me for much of mine. This injunction was reinforced by the way I interpreted what I learned in church: that the purpose of life's journey is to "move on to perfection." I bought into this notion, so much so that I spent way too much time and energy presenting an idealized view of myself to the world, including those I led, even while knowing I was not being authentic. Perhaps you have done something similar: hidden weaknesses, denied prejudices, ignored limits, pretended knowledge, not owned or expressed "bad" feelings, avoided conflict, to name a few examples. I am slowly learning that the purpose of my journey is not to be perfect but to be "perfectly Russ," which for me now means "becoming the person I started out to be"—a whole and authentic person.

Charles Handy wrote about his story of living as a false self. A well-known business writer, Handy was an executive with Shell Oil and was one of the first faculty members of the London Business School. In *The Hungry Spirit,* Handy wrote:

> I spent the early part of my life trying to be someone else. At school I wanted to be a great athlete, at the university an admired socialite, after-wards a businessman, and, later, the head of a great institution. It did not take me long to realize that I was not to be successful in any of these guises, but that did not prevent me from trying, and from being perpet-ually disappointed with myself. The problem was in trying to be some-one else I neglected to concentrate on the person I could be. I was happier going along with the conventions of the time, measuring success in terms of money and position, climbing ladders that others placed in my way, collecting things and contacts, rather than giving expression to my own beliefs and personality. I was, in retrospect, hiding from myself [1998, p. 79].

One of the guises we put on is the identity of someone else. In the middle of a one-to-one coaching session a bright and high potential middle manager, Robert, said to me, "I love to read, and every time I read another book about an effective leader I think I must be just like him." He had read recent biographies about Jack Welch and Rudy Giu-liani and he had attempted to be like them, to do what they did in the way they did it, in his leadership role. Rather than become himself, Robert wanted to become another Welch or Giuliani. "It took me a while to realize," Robert said, "that I could not be like them, and that I did not need to be like them. I needed to be me."

A clergy leader, Norman, told a similar story. "In the first several years after seminary I thought if I were to be successful I needed to imitate the effective and successful leaders I knew. I thought of the clergy leaders I admired, remembered what they did in particular situations, and tried doing the same thing. I remember how one set direction for his church, how he introduced new ideas, and I tried to do it the same way. I even noticed and tried to imitate some of his gestures. It took time to recognize that trying to be like someone else prevented me from being the person I was."

Norman and Robert are not unique. Many of us read stories of larger-than-life leaders like Giuliani and Welch, or observe other leaders we admire, and think we must be like them if we are to be effective. We are "wannabes"; we try to imitate others, we try on their faces to see if they will fit us. Instead of becoming the person we started out to be, we try to become someone else. While it is important we learn from other leaders we admire, the point is to become and be our self.

Another way we show up as a false self is by trying to develop traits like charisma, even when it is not part of who we are. I love politics and enjoy watching political leaders like Eric. Eric was a thoughtful and cerebral type; his positions on important economic and social issues were thoughtfully considered and carefully crafted. I imagined him to be an introvert, a man who would not make statements until he had thought them through. But I did not think of him as having charisma.

I attended one of his political rallies. At the start of the rally Eric quietly made his way through the crowd, making good connections with individuals, listening attentively to them, responding helpfully and appropriately to what they said. His gifts were on display in these one-to-one interactions. Then he moved to the stage for a fist-pumping, joke-telling campaign speech. On stage he tried to exhibit charisma, but he didn't seem comfortable doing it. He wasn't being himself. He lost the election. I cannot tell you he would have won had he been the same person on-stage that he was off, but I do know authenticity is one of the important things I look for in any political candidate.

Eric worked hard to develop, or at least display, charisma even when it was simply not who he was. I suspect it was the guise he thought he needed. It is a trait that many leaders think they must have because, as one executive said to me recently, "all effective leaders have it." Though there is scant evidence in the literature linking charisma to leadership success, and some well-researched books like Jim Collins' *From Good to Great* suggest there is no link at all between the two, the belief that it is important still persists. There is nothing wrong with traits like charisma per se; the problem comes when we wear them as we would wear an ill-fitting suit of clothes. When the trait does not fit who we are, it is better to leave it in the closet.

One more story. I joined the management development staff of a large corporation about the time that *In Search of Excellence*, by Tom Peters and Robert Waterman, was published. Among other things, Peters and Waterman encouraged individuals to "manage by walking around" (MBWA). A good idea, as techniques go. But the problem is that the technique does not fit the basic identity of every person. One manager in our department had a gift for small talk, was comfortable dropping by a cubicle or office for a quick chat, and used MBWA effectively to focus attention and keep the department's agenda front and center. MBWA allowed him to express his true self. Another manager was rather shy, did not engage easily or well in casual banter, tended to be more formal, and worked more effectively in scheduled meetings that had a planned agenda. He thought he should try to manage by walking around—it was, after all, the technique of the day—but MBWA was not a way for him to express his real self. It was awkward for him and awkward for those of us he managed. Techniques like MBWA are useful and helpful when—and only when—they help us express our authentic self.

We have a choice. Trappist monk Thomas Merton describes our choice this way: "We can be ourselves or not, as we please. We are at liberty to be real, or to be unreal. We may be true or false, the choice is ours. We may wear one mask and now another and never, if we so desire, appear with our own true face. But we cannot make these choices with impunity.... Every one of us is shadowed by an illusory person: a false self. This is the man I want to be but who cannot exist ... we are not very good at recognizing illusions, least of all the ones we cherish about ourselves ... for most people in this world there is no greater subjective reality that this false sense of theirs" (1961, pp. 31, 32).

It is easy to think that a false self is a bad self. But the false self I created—my idealized self—wasn't a bad self, it just wasn't my real self. I now think of it as an important step—in the language of Richard Rohr a "necessary warm-up act"—to my becoming myself. I crafted or created this false self because at the time I needed it. What I did not know was that in "wearing one mask and then another" I would learn more about my own "true face." I am becoming myself not in spite of having a false self, but precisely and partially because of it.

We can be an inauthentic self rather than a true self. In a way, being inauthentic may sound like another way of being a false self. It could even be argued that the distinction between being an inauthentic self and being a false self is a distinction without a difference. But to add granularity to my premise, I suggest that there is an important difference between the two. Showing up as a false self says that our leadership is not rooted in our core identity; instead, we think the false self we have carefully crafted is our real or core self. In contrast, showing up as an inauthentic self happens when we know who we are in our core—we know our real and true self—but we act in ways that violate this self.

Everywhere we turn these days we read or see stories of individuals who do not lead with integrity—leaders who are jailed for illegal conduct, executives who rob employees of their retirement and steal their security, elected officials who become so used to spinning that the real truth gets lost, and church leaders and youth-serving leaders who abuse their position of trust and hurt those they were meant to serve.

But this is not just true for "them"; it is also true for "us." Consider the evidence that all of us act in inauthentic ways:

- In a leadership team meeting we want to say "no" to a decision being made or a direction taken but say "yes" instead.
- We realize—even if only faintly—that the values we espouse are not the values we live.
- We do not speak our truth to others or share our convictions with others, especially those in positions of power, and then we blame them for our lack of forthrightness—after all, they will shoot the messenger, won't they?
- We hide our important and defining beliefs when the heat is on.
- We make a presentation to our organization's leadership team and realize right in the middle of it that we are sharing just the data we think they want to hear.

- We participate in cooking the books—literally and metaphorically —knowing all the while it is wrong.
- We slowly realize the work we do and the life we lead are not our own, that we are not authoring our own life. We have a name for why we continue to do it: "the golden handcuffs."
- We hate spin and yet we spin the truth. The difference is that when we do it there is always a good reason, or so we tell ourselves.
- We wake up one day and realize our soul is disconnected from our role, that who we are is not connected to what we do. This realization is painful.

Jerry Harvey, a professor at George Washington University and a well-known author, tells us in *The Abilene Paradox and Other Meditations on Management* that collusion undermines organizational effectiveness. What's collusion? Simply stated, it is saying yes when we want to say no. It is saying we agree to a new vision for our organization when we have real doubts; it is saying we agree to a new strategic direction when we actually think it will take us the wrong way on a one-way street; it is voting "aye" to a change initiative when inside we feel real resistance. The result: decisions are made without all the critical input available and without the support needed to succeed, and the organization winds up going to Abilene (a place nobody really wanted to go).

Acting in inauthentic ways—whether "they" do it or "we" do it—always cause pain. It causes personal pain; it tears at the fabric of relationships; it undermines organizational effectiveness; and it exacts a horrible cost to society. When politicians spin, when executives "tell the truth and nothing but the truth" and then are convicted, when church leaders cover up and we collude, trust is lost and cynicism grows. Distrust and cynicism are not the right foundation on which good relationships, enduring organizations, or great communities and nations are built.

We can be ego-self rather than a whole and authentic self. Having a strong and healthy ego is important; especially for those engaged in leadership. It helps leaders know what is real, and adapt to that reality. It helps leaders stay grounded.

Individuals engaged in leadership activities must have a full measure of self-confidence or ego-strength. They must believe in their ability to perform in high-pressure situations; they must have the backbone needed to handle tough situations; they must be resilient enough to bounce back from mistakes and failures. Conversely, they must not be riddled with self-doubt.

But true self is different than ego self. I began to understand this difference from the writings of Carl Jung, the famed Swedish psychoanalyst. For Jung, ego was one aspect of "Self." The "Self" embraces and includes the ego, but it is more than ego. The problem is that "most people confuse 'self knowledge' with knowledge of their conscious ego personalities. Anyone who has any ego consciousness takes it for granted that he knows himself. But the ego only knows its own content ... what is called self knowledge is a very limited knowledge" (2006, p. 309). We think we know ourselves, but we actually only know a part of ourselves, especially if what we know is limited to what is in our conscious awareness. It is easy to become victims of our ego consciousness.

A second problem is that a healthy ego, which is necessary for effective leadership, can and often does become supersized. An individual in a leadership role with a supersized ego focuses on his or her own wants and needs rather than the needs of others or the needs of the organization. However fine the line, when a manager or executive goes from having self-confidence to becoming egocentric, there are serious negative consequences, and not only for the person's performance, but for the impact she will have on others and the organization.

What I have noticed, and perhaps you have also, is that the trip up the organizational ladder can be intoxicating, encouraging healthy egos to become supersized. The ascent—and the increasing array of perks associated with it—pushes those who start with a lot of self-confidence over the line into egocentric behaviors. Like Narcissus of Greek legend, executives who are not careful are prone to fall in love with their own image, and confuse this image with their authentic self.

One of the most interesting executives with whom I have worked was a man of towering intellect, an engaging and warm sense of humor, and a person extremely confident of his knowledge and ability. He had enough "starch in his collar"—enough ego strength—to tackle the toughest, most difficult problems and offer bold ideas for the organization's future. He was honored for his work. By the time I got to know him, two walls of his office were covered with plaques acknowledging one contribution or another, or pictures of him with various dignitaries. He enjoyed regaling people with stories of positions he had held, people he had known, and confrontations he had won with his board. After a while I began to wonder who he was beyond the "brag walls"; I wondered if he knew. I began thinking that perhaps he had fallen in love with an image.

Our journey to becoming our self—our true, authentic self—includes developing a healthy ego, but does not stop there. Our journey takes us past our ego to our true and authentic self.

We can be a fragmented or separated self rather than a whole self. There are a lot of ways we attempt to compartmentalize life, to keep one part of ourselves separate from another. We think we need to do this. Others expect if from us, or so we tell ourselves, and we have learned to expect it from ourselves.

True self is composed of four energies or domains: the physical, the mental, the emotional, and the spiritual. The four energies are inter-dependent; our wholeness requires that they be integrated. But in our business and personal lives we work hard to keep these domains separate and apart.

We know that our workplaces require mental energy. We use it to envision the future, plan strategies that will help us move in a desired direction, analyze results, solve pressing problems, and make decisions. We also move, sit, travel, and work long hours, all of which require the use of physical energy.

But we tell ourselves, and we are told, that there is not room for emotions in the rational world of work—not in decision-making, not in strategic planning, and certainly not in the way we decide to treat employees, as evidenced by cold, impersonal employee handbooks full of standard operating procedures, or in the way we typically downsize organizations—showing a longtime employee to the door accompanied by an escort. We forget that emotion and motivation come from the same root word, and that it is how we feel about something more than the thing itself that is motivating or de-motivating. Spiritual energy is better left for the church or mosque or synagogue to handle, or so we seem to think, forgetting that spiritual energy is what gives meaning and purpose to the work we do.

2. Becoming a Leader Is Becoming Yourself

A second way we attempt to keep our lives compartmentalized is that we try to keep our public self separated from our private self. Carl Jung told us that there is a difference in our public self, the self we want others to see and that we are pleased to present to the public, and our shadow self, that part of us we do not like and hope that others won't notice. Because we don't like what lurks in our shadow, we try to keep it under wraps, by either hiding it or controlling it. But we simply cannot fragment ourselves, no matter how hard we try. It is a bound-to-happen kind of thing that the insecurities, doubts or the just-below-the-surface anger that we think we can hide surfaces at the wrong time to hurt others and haunt us.

Several years ago, I worked as a coach with an executive who was responsible for a huge part of his company's operation. He was a brilliant individual, knowledgeable, forceful, and by all external measures successful. Away from work he was fun to be with; I always looked forward to our lunches or dinners together. The feedback I had gathered about him as part of the coaching process suggested that he was confident and self-assured; that he made hard decisions in a timely way, that he confronted those whose work was not up to par, even took on corporate when he disagreed with a decision or direction handed down. But I also gathered interview data from his boss, his colleagues and his direct reports that suggested he was insecure. As I worked with him and observed him in action, I noticed how often he needed to let others know that he was *the* boss. I saw the ways he kept others, including me, in a one-down position (he expected compliance not collaboration), and I became aware of how he used coercive power to get his way. I began to realize the interview data was accurate and if I could peel back the layers of the onion far enough, I would find an insecure and threatened man. To the extent he knew this about himself he tried to keep it hidden. But it did not stay hidden, and when it surfaced it was not benign. It was toxic for him, and it poisoned important work relationships.

We'll examine our shadow selves more in a later chapter, but for now it is important to remember that though it is a hard, difficult journey to take to go down and in and face, then integrate, the insecurities, fears, and anger that lurk deep inside, we cannot be whole men and women, and engage in leadership fully and wholly, unless we do.

45

So What Is True Self?

If effective leadership is rooted in our wholeness and authenticity, the important next question is, "how will we know our whole and authentic self when we see it?" Who are we on the other side of ego self, false self, inauthentic self, and fragmented self? The following points to some early clues.

True self is the "person we started out to be." As T.S. Eliot said so beautifully, "And at the end of all our exploring / will be to arrive where we started / and know the place for the first time." No one starts out to be inauthentic, to hide him or herself, to be someone else. Just the opposite is true: we start out as whole, integral people—it is who we were and who we long to once again be. It is how we were born, and our hope is that on our journey we will make our way back to "arrive where we started."

True self is the self that exists on the other side of false self. The false self is the self we construct to satisfy others; it is the self that we think will be acceptable; it is the self we think others expect us to be; it is an idealized self. Too often, though, we come to believe that false self is the fundamental reality.

Becoming our true self requires that you and I get to know that self that lives underneath the externals, beyond the titles, the "brag wall," the trappings of success, the power and prestige that are related solely to position in a hierarchy. It requires that we get past all the doing—doing that unfortunately provides many of us our identity—to discover who we are at the center of our being. Here's the question: when you peel back the layers of the proverbial onion, who are you at your core?

True self is a wholly human self. Earlier I wrote about my need to present an idealized image of myself to others. I wanted others to look at me as someone who had his act together. I refused to admit fears, or insecurities, or prejudices. I had a hard time saying "I don't know." I tried hard not to show anger or other so-called negative emotions. What I have slowly learned is that the purpose of my life journey, and my leadership journey, is not to be perfect, but to be wholly and perfectly human. For me this means acknowledging that I have gifts and limits, that I cast light and shadow, that I have doubts or sometimes simply don't know, and that I make mistakes and hurt others. I am learning that when I acknowledge these things I am more trusted and am seen as more effective.

True self is a whole and integrated self. We move toward becoming a whole person when we understand the inextricable link between all of our energies, when we integrate inner life and outer work, when we befriend and embrace our shadow, when we discern and own our gifts and our limits. When engaged in accomplishing the tasks of leadership, the more we integrate all the different parts of ourselves, the more creativity and energy we unleash and the more value we create both inside and outside the organization.

Leadership Tasks and Becoming Our True Selves

In the first chapter, leadership is defined as the accomplishment of three critical tasks: *crafting a vision or clear sense direction for an organization, community, or country; creating alignment with that vision and maintaining commitment to it.* The leadership bottom-line: when these three tasks are accomplished effective leadership has happened.

In this chapter I argue that being an effective leader does not require grafting traits like charisma onto one's personality. Leadership is not based on having the right set of tips and techniques and does not result from using some tried and true recipe, but instead is rooted in the authenticity and wholeness of the leader.

Earlier, I suggested that leadership is everyone's vocation. We are past the time when it is helpful to think that "they" are the leaders and "we" are the followers. Today we need a new understanding of leadership that says, clearly, we are all leaders and followers.

This chapter has discussed that we each have gifts and skills and energies to offer to the accomplishment of leadership tasks. I really believe this. What is required is that we show up as authentic and whole men and women—as true self, make our distinctive contribution to the accomplishment of leadership tasks, and accept our responsibility for the outcomes.

When authentic and whole men and women come together to

accomplish leadership tasks, any organization can maximize its potential and become the best it can be.

Becoming True Self Is a Journey

Warren Bennis had it exactly right in one more way. He said: "you must, in sum, *become* the person you started out to be." He did *not* say "*be* the person you started out to be." This small distinction is of huge importance. It points us to another premise of this book: becoming true self is a process, a journey, a journey back to who we started out to be. The journey to recovering that which is most original and most personal in ourselves is the focus of the next chapter.

But one important reality of the journey needs to be mentioned now: we do not embark on this journey for ourselves alone. It is a not another navel-gazing narcissistic exercise in self-aggrandizement. It is not another way to "get a leg up" on others or to better position oneself for future career opportunities, including opportunities to engage in leadership. It is not, as some suggest, selfish to spend time on this journey; learning to know and love oneself counteracts narcissism rather than encourages it. When you become the person you started out to be you can truly offer your "gifts and skills and energies" to the practice of leadership. When you become yourself you can engage in leadership in authentic and life-giving ways.

3. The Journey Home

There was a time, five years ago or so, that my wife, Jean, and I were wandering through one of the lovely mountain communities that dot the map in the western part of North Carolina when, out of the corner of my eye, I spotted in a store window a rugged wooden picture frame, with a map in the background, a house in the foreground, and this saying around the edge: *life is a journey back to home.*

I said to Jean: that's not just the life journey; it is also the journey leaders must take.

Returning home has, for me, become a metaphor for returning to whole and authentic self. Sue Monk Kidd also uses this metaphor and writes, "The image of coming home is a powerful, archetypal symbol of returning to one's deepest self, to the soul. To return home is to return to the place of inner origin ... we all have this profound longing to come home ... perhaps the root spiritual problem of our time is that modern people have lost their way home. Not only that, we've lost directions to find it. There are few places within our scientific, rationalistic culture that have enough connection to the symbolic realm of soul to point the way.... Without maps and signposts, people search for home in the wrong places: in professional success, material status, institutions ... but none of these can ever be home. We are spiritual refugees" (1990, pp. 89, 90).

This journey home is a difficult one. There are no roadmaps to help us find our way. MapQuest cannot provide accurate directions. There are no high-speed superhighways that can get us there in a hurry. Not even those who know us best and love us deeply can give us the right direction for our travels, though there are other ways they can be helpful to us.

It is a different kind of journey. It takes us toward home, not away from it. It takes us to the place we started and to the person we started out to be, not to somewhere else or someone new. In fact, it does not take us anywhere out there, rather it takes us in and down to a place where we confront some of the most important realities of life. This journey is not a vacation.

Even more problematic, we may have spent so much time "wearing other people's faces" that we have a hard time recognizing our own. We may have spent so much energy trying to be the person others wanted or expected us to be, or we thought we ought to be, and we have lost touch with the person we are.

But here's life's promise: if you take the journey faithfully, you will find your way home and become the person you started out to be. When this happens you will be able to engage in leadership as a whole and authentic person.

Why the Journey Is Needed

But first, the question: why take this journey? Why are we not adequate exactly as we are? Why shouldn't we simply accept who we are and leave it at that?

Over the years I have been privileged to work with many managers and executives from all types of organizations—business leaders, non-profit leaders, civic leaders, educational leaders, and clergy leaders. Because of their positions, all were engaged in and responsible for seeing that leadership tasks were accomplished in their organizations. By and large, they took this responsibility seriously. Most were successful.

What it usually means to be successful is to do well in the external world—the world of numerical growth, of new program development, of accomplishing strategic direction and successfully navigating change. The founder and owner of a very successful retail business told me, "If you can't measure it, you can't manage it." This is the world in which a lot of leaders live—a world of objective, external measures, measures that allow outside observers to determine who is successful and who isn't. We have been led to believe that success can be determined in just this way—in schools success is determined if no child is left behind, in nonprofit organizations by funds raised and by memberships increased, and in businesses by return to stockholders.

3. The Journey Home

Some individuals thrive in this external world and it doesn't occur to them that there might be something missing. But there is an increasing number of men and women who are successful, and yet long for something more, something different in life. They long to return home. They know they are refugees and they don't like it.

For much of my life I have been one of these refugees. As suggested in the last chapter, I have spent too much of my life, and too much of my energy, trying to present an idealized image of myself to others. I wanted others to think of me as someone who had his act together, even though deep inside I was full of doubts and insecurities. My worst fear was that others would find out I was an impostor. So I hid my fears, covered my weaknesses, denied my self-doubt—or so I thought. Slowly, and over time, I realized that maintaining an image is too hard and not really necessary. I longed to return home.

I have worked with refugees. Several years ago I was serving as an executive coach to one of the leaders of a company. As part of this assignment I collected a massive amount of information about his strengths and weaknesses, gifts, and limits, and had scheduled a half-day meeting to "unpack" this data with him. Before we started looking at the data, he asked if we could just talk. I said sure. In essence, he said: "I am doing better than I ever imagined I would do. I am at a higher level in this organization than I ever considered possible, have more perks than I imagined possible, and have more power than I want or need. By most standards I am successful. But I am miserable." He went on to tell me that the happiest he had been was early in his career when he was doing work where his gifts and skills were used, work he found deeply satisfying. That work, he said, was his calling. But his organization identified him as high potential, put the hierarchical ladder in front of him and encouraged him to climb it. Being considered high potential and encouraged to think of oneself as having the right stuff to be an executive was heady —it was such a fine seduction that it would be difficult, if not impossible, for him or anyone else to refuse. This executive allowed himself to be seduced, only later to realize that the ladder the organization asked him to climb was against the wrong wall. He also realized that he was playing a role rather than becoming and being the person he started out to be. He was experiencing the pain of being a refugee.

Just recently I heard a similar story from a clergy leader with whom

I have worked. While in seminary he was encouraged to pursue a doctorate in theology. He was told that he had the "right stuff" to succeed academically and he had important contributions to make to the field of Biblical studies. Though he felt called to serve the local church, he did as he was encouraged and enrolled in a doctoral program. In his own words, "I spent my days in the library when my call was to serve people. I am an extrovert, get energy from being with people, and I found time spent in the library to be draining—I was going against my call and against my grain to try to become the person others thought I should be." This good man found his way back home; at least for now he is not a refugee. He is now serving as pastor of a local church, loves his life and his ministry, and is fulfilled by it.

This is the same story that I have heard from countless others who discover, often belatedly, that the ladder they climbed and the life they lived were not their own. I heard a story from an engineer who wondered how and why she became "high potential" when what she wanted was to be a "high professional" in her engineering role. This is also true for the sales professional who loved "doing deals" but found himself managing others who did the work he loved, the competent and caring teacher who was encouraged to become an administrator only to realize her heart was in the classroom, and the organizational leader who realized she could not be fulfilled or effective by emulating others she admired. These men and women experienced the pain of living far from home. They longed to once again become the person they started out to be.

I have heard similar stories from countless men and women who spent their life in hiding, who showed up at work with their "game face" on, who colluded with decisions made or directions taken that they knew were wrong, who looked the other way when unethical behavior was treated with a wink and a nod, or who knew that the "monsters" lurking in their shadow—their insecurities, their anger, their fears—were impacting their practice of leadership but did nothing to change it.

You and I decide to take the journey to being whole and authentic when we realize we cannot find our true self in any exterior place, whether it is a role, a title, a position of power, whatever. We will *never* find our true self there.

Or we decide to take the journey home when we tire of being spiritual refugees. We long to experience ourselves as whole and authentic. We decide it is time to move past false self and ego self to true self, to show up wearing our own face, and to act with a deep sense of integrity. We decide to become the person we started out to be.

All the great spiritual traditions offer hope that wholeness is possible, but it has been my personal experience, and the experience of others whose stories I know, that the journey toward true self—toward whole and authentic self—is one we often avoid until some crisis leaves us dissolved and shaken.

Crises as Catalyst for the Journey

One of the most difficult realities about the journey to true self is that it often takes a crisis to turn us toward home. Crises are precursors if not prerequisites to our becoming our self.

Poet May Sarton suggests that on the journey to ourselves we will be "dissolved and shaken" (1993). Authors Warren Bennis and Robert Thomas say it is "crucible" experiences that shape leaders and change them in some fundamental way (2002). Franciscan priest Richard Rohr writes that it is "fallings and failings" and "necessary sufferings" that propel us past false self to true self (2011). In research done at the Center for Creative Leadership, organizational leaders say it is hardship experiences from which they learn the most enduring life and leadership lessons (Moxley and Pulley 2004).

Disintegration, dissolution, disappearance, disturbance, and disequilibria are synonyms that we might use to describe our experience during hardships, while in the crucible, or when we are failing and falling. It is hard to fathom that experiences like these are part of the process of becoming whole and authentic. We would avoid such experiences if we could. We would like to find an alternate, easier route to becoming ourselves. In a workshop I attended author and consultant Peter Block said, "We all want to get to heaven but none of us want to die." While not all of us will experience the harshness of dissolution, none of us are exempt from the experience of hardships. There are no free rides.

Part Two: The Journey to Authentic Leadership

During the years I served as a full-time faculty member at the Center for Creative Leadership one of the important research project undertaken was a look at how executive men and women develop their leadership skills and perspectives over time. The results of the research, now replicated four times with different populations, are clear and convincing—individuals can develop some of the leadership skills they need (they have gifts; they develop skills) and they can learn them from a variety of experiences: facing challenging assignments, working with other people who provide support, feedback and challenge, learning from an array of training events and coursework, leadership experiences outside of work, and hardships. In the last replication of the research hardship experiences were mentioned more than any other single event as the experience from which women and men learned the most enduring leadership lessons.

A story makes this point clear. I worked with the executive team of a large consumer products company to help them think about how they would identify and develop the next generation of leaders for their organization. Rather than simply share with them data from CCL's research, I started with the original research question: "When you think about your career, certain events or episodes probably stand out, events that caused a change in the way you manage today. Please identify three of those key events." Members of the executive team responded with expected answers: jobs in which they felt stretched and had to learn new skills to survive, bad bosses and good mentors, and life experiences unrelated to their actual work. Jim, the president and general manager, didn't respond until he was coaxed into doing so by the chief legal counsel of the company. Somewhat reluctantly he described two of the key events he had listed: his bypass surgery and his wife's battle with breast cancer. He recounted in clear and concrete ways how these painful experiences had changed him and his practice of management and leadership. The other members of the senior leadership team, all present at this gathering, confirmed that these two events had made him a more trust-based, less hierarchical, more compassionate—yet no less demanding—executive.

One of my favorite stories in Biblical literature is the story of the Prodigal Son. It is an archetypal story, and here is my version of it: a younger son in a family asks his father for the share of the inheritance that belongs to him, and the father obliges. Soon after the "younger son gathered all he had and took a journey into a far country, and there he squandered his property in loose living." (RSV, p. 87). After losing everything a great famine arose and this younger son was hungry and began to hurt. He was a refugee and was living far from home, literally and metaphorically. He found work with a citizen who sent him into the fields to feed the pigs. The son was so hungry he would have gladly eaten the corncobs the pigs ate, but no one gave him anything. It is at this point—in the middle of a very real crisis—that the son "came to himself." After coming to himself—his true self, to use our language—he began his journey home, and when he arrived he found his father waiting for him with open arms.

Notice the steps in this journey: the younger son lived at home; he chose to exile himself in a far country; he lost a sense of his truest and deepest self; he squandered his inheritance and his life; he experienced real hardship; during the hardship experience he "came to himself" and turned toward home. The phrase "he came to himself" suggests that this younger son somehow knew that he wasn't being himself—not his whole or authentic self—while he was squandering his inheritance in loose living and later when he found himself feeding the swine. He was not being his true self and he knew it, and for him, as for us, the experience of hardship was the catalyst for turning toward home.

These may just be the steps each of us takes on the journey—literally and metaphorically: we start at home, leave it, experience hardship, and turn back toward home. For certain, it is a journey I have taken, and more than once. The hope for us when we are wandering in a far country is that we will know, somehow, that we are not being the person we started out to be, and that our "failing and falling" will propel us forward, not defeat us, that we will come to ourselves, and begin the journey home.

The father, when his son returned home, said, "he once was dead and now is alive, was lost and now is found." Dead and alive. Lost and found. We start out at home. We get lost. We feel dead. We find our self again. We feel alive.

In the last chapter I suggested there are many fine seductions in the places we work that are distorting, that can bend us out shape, from the climb up the corporate ladder to the projections and expectations of others, to our own attempts to be like those leaders we admire and want to emulate. We get lost, or at least our true self gets buried beneath the layers. Then hardship happens and we are shaken, often to the core. We begin the process of finding the way home to our deeper and truer selves.

There is an older brother in this story of the prodigal son who shows us we can stay at home, literally, but still lose our true self. When the younger son arrived home and was warmly embraced by the father, this older son was working in the fields. When he had finished his work and was walking home he heard the celebration at the house. He asked a servant what the music and dancing meant, and when he was told the father had killed a fatted calf and was preparing a feast because the younger brother was safe and at home, the older brother got angry and sulked off. He later confronted his father and bitterly complained that he had been obedient all his life and yet he had never been given a "kid" to share with his friends.

My religious self is one of my least attractive false selves. I am obedient. I do what I think is right. At times I work hard in my version of the "field," though it is not work I really want to do. Too often I expect to be rewarded, and expect those like the younger brother to be punished. At these times I am self-righteous and judgmental, and I sulk when I do not get my way. Thankfully, I have learned that this is not the self I was created to be, and it is not the self I uncover as I journey past ego self to true self. But the point is clear and important: sometimes even the most well-meaning among us mistake being good and righteous with being whole and authentic.

The Center for Creative Leadership has identified six categories of hardships. In these categories the crises of the company executive and the prodigal son are called "personal trauma." The others include business mistakes and failures, being passed over for a promotion or stuck in a lousy job, dealing with difficult people, breaking a rut (taking a risk by leaving a comfortable job for a new and more challenging one) and, from the last replication of the research, a new category has emerged called "differences matter" (the reality that being a minority because of gender or race is, in and of itself, a hardship). Each hardship was accompanied by a particular experience of loss. When the hardship was a demotion or a downsizing, it was a loss of identity. When the hardship was a mistake or failure, or being passed over for a promotion, it was a loss of self-efficacy. It is the experience of loss that drives learning.

Warren Bennis and Robert Thomas discovered a similar dynamic from their own research, which they reported on in the *Harvard Business Review*. They wrote: "Our recent research has led us to conclude that one of the most reliable indicators and predictors of true leadership is an individual's ability to find meaning in negative events and learn from even the most trying circumstances ... we came to call these experiences that shape leaders "crucibles" ... the crucible experience was a trial and a test, a point of deep self-reflection that forced them [the 40 individuals interviewed] to question who they were and what mattered to them ... invariably, they emerged from the crucible stronger and more sure of themselves and their purpose—changed in some fundamental way" (2002, pp. 5, 6). In the crucible our ego is deconstructed, which allows crucible experiences to change us in a fundamental way. When this happens we begin to see ourselves with fresh eyes. Hardships help us move beyond ego to the center of our being.

In a commencement address delivered at Stanford University, Steve Jobs described crucible experiences that turned him toward home. He told "three stories from my life. That's it. No big deal. Just three stories." The second story was about "love and loss"—starting, building, and then getting fired from Apple Computer, all in a space of ten years. Jobs said, "What had been the focus of my entire adult life was gone; and it was devastating. I really did not know what to do for a few months ... I didn't see it then, but it turned out that getting fired from Apple was the best thing that could have ever happened to me. The heaviness of being successful was replaced by the lightness of being a beginner again ... during the next five years I started a company named NeXT and another company named Pixar ... I am pretty sure none of this would have happened if I hadn't been fired from Apple. It was awful-tasting medicine, but I guess the patient needed it. Sometimes life hits you in the head with a brick. Don't lose faith" (2005, pp. 31, 32).

For a long time I rejected the notion that falling down and failing were necessary catalysts for my turning toward home. I didn't think I needed "awful-tasting medicine." I grew up in a church that promotes "moving on to perfection," in a culture that prizes upward mobility, and in a country in which "progress is our most important product." In my years growing up no one told me that hardship and crises were an important part of the journey, or that I could learn some of the more important leadership and life lessons from experiencing them.

But off and on over the years I have thought a lot about the hardships I have experienced and the mistakes I have made—mistakes made in personal relationships and in leadership roles. For example, my lack of courage, my unwillingness to act on my core values, my tendency to say "yes" when I wanted to say "no" were all mistakes I thought of as bad and I regretted making them—in some ways and at various times, I still do. They can and do haunt me. But I have a growing realization that these fallings and failings have changed me in fundamental ways, that who I am today, at least in part, is because of the mistakes, not in spite of them. My mistakes have placed my footsteps on the only way home. This is what crises large and small do for each of us.

Hardship and loss is a catalyst for learning, but learning is not automatic. For Steve Jobs and the corporate president who described his illness and his wife's cancer as the experiences in which he learned the most enduring leadership lessons, it was the willingness to face the hardships, accept responsibility for them, and learn from them that was important. Like these two leaders, each of us will experience crises in the course of our life. Though it will be different for each of us, we will know the meaning of being "dissolved and shaken." But we learn that the crisis is not the end of the story. Poet William Stafford offers reassurance about what is possible: "you live in a world where stumbling / always leads home" (1998, p. 7). It is easy to focus on the stumbling, on the mistakes made, on the wrong turns taken, or on the personal traumas experienced. It is easy to be thrown off track by them. It is possible to be defeated by them. But the reassuring truth is that stumbling always leads us home.

The Journey Takes Us In and Down

Another difficult aspect of the journey to true self and authentic leadership is that it takes us inward to some of the hardest realities of life, not outward to some exotic locale. We do not find home by looking "out there," rather it is found by looking "in here." If we summon the courage to take the inner journey and we will find our core, the center of our being, the place in which our true self is rooted. When we find it, we also will find solid ground on which to stand and lead.

Discovering this solid ground is not easy. It is far easier to live with the illusion that there is something "out there" that we can fix or set straight to make things right. It is easy to believe that the source of any trouble we experience is outside of us. If we change jobs, change relationships, or change locations, we can start over, or so we seem to think.

For sure, going in and down has not been easy for me. By preference and temperament, I am a person who likes reality that can be measured and observed. I prefer data that can be known to one of my senses. I take clues from my external environment. I learned to live outside of myself, and was rewarded for doing it. After years of journeying, with my share of crises, I am much more aware of how important it is find my inner ground and stay firmly rooted there.

I learned this the hard way. After several years on the training and development staff of a company in Dallas I transferred to another of the corporation's operating companies, this one headquartered in Anchorage, Alaska. The transfer was also a promotion; in Anchorage I was manager of management and organization development. For the first time in my career I would have, in a formal sense, direct reports. I was eager to see if I could apply the skills and perspectives I had taught in workshops to the actual practice of managing people. With one of these direct reports I experienced the hardship that CCL labeled "dealing with difficult people." He was a brilliant, insightful internal consultant on some occasions and a manipulative, dishonest power broker on others. But this is not a story about him, it is a story about me and the struggle I had giving him honest feedback on those occasions when his behavior undermined our group's credibility in the larger organization. I knew the skills of giving feedback. I had taught them countless times to others, even demonstrated them in role-play situations. I would rehearse what I wanted to say to this employee, using all the language and techniques I had been teaching to others. But when it came time for a face-to-face conversation my need for approval and affection was stronger than my determination to speak my truth. I had many of the same issues and problems as other managers and executives whom I had been training in performance appraisal workshops. I did not engage with him with authenticity or integrity. I did not stand on the solid ground of my identity. I lacked sufficient courage. My inner life affected my outer work; on my journey to true and whole self I have had to wrestle with these inner life issues.

During this same time I went to a workshop led by Peter Block, one of my favorite leadership thinkers, writers, and consultants. His keen insights have nourished me throughout my career. In this workshop Peter and his colleague, Joel Henning, had us develop a vision for ourselves and for the organization we led. After creating the vision Peter asked us to name the fear and/or dependency need that would keep us from accomplishing it. The assumption was that it was something "in here," not anything "out there," that would keep us from fulfilling our deepest hopes for ourselves and our organization. Interestingly, I had no trouble naming mine; neither did the other participants in the workshop. When we took time to look, we could all see how our inner life affected our outer work.

Carl Jung named the difference between inner and outer life in a helpful way when he distinguished between our public persona and our shadow self. But, as I have learned from my own experience in life and leadership activities, I cannot keep my shadow hidden or in the dark—it shows itself at the wrong times with the wrong people. It was my need for approval and some of my dependency needs, both part of my shadow, which I identified as things that would keep me from fulfilling my deepest hopes for my organization.

All people have a shadow, but organizational leaders are in a position where the shadow they cast is a longer one. I will talk more about the concept of shadow in the next chapter; for now, it is important to note that in the journey home we must travel down and in to acknowledge, embrace, and then integrate our shadow into our lives or else we will always be at the mercy of its untimely and unfortunate appearances.

There Is No Clear Path

Literally and metaphorically, it is always easier to start a journey when we have sure knowledge of our destination and clear directions for how to get there. But the journey to true self isn't like this. There are no clear directions and only a few travel aids. Joseph Campbell once wrote that if we could clearly see the path laid out in front of us, we could know for certain it was not our path.

Because there is no clear path, the journey requires a lifelong commitment to personal observation, personal discovery, and personal growth. Along the way there will be dead-ends and detours. The wrong road will be taken or, to use an earlier analogy, the wrong ladder will be climbed. Some may veer off track or even get lost. Along the way some paths will close and others open, new interests will be stirred, new gifts will be discerned and a new calling may be heard. Life emerges or unfolds, as much if not more than is planned. The path is found, or created, as we journey.

I love how Jayber Crow, the barber/philosopher in the book by poet and novelist Wendell Berry, described his journey:

> If you could do it, I suppose, it would be a good idea to live your life in a straight line—starting say in the Dark Wood of Error, and proceeding by logical steps through Hell and Purgatory and into Heaven. Or you could take the King's Highway past appropriately named dangers, toils and snares, and finally across the River of Death and enter the Celestial City. But that is not the way I have done it, so far. I am a pilgrim, but my pilgrimage has been wandering and unmarked. Often what looked like a straight line has been a circle or a doubling back. I have been in the Dark Wood of Error any number of times. I have known something of Hell, Purgatory and Heaven, but not always in that order. The names of many snares and dangers have been made known to me, but I have seen them only in looking back. Often I have not known where I was going until I was already there. I have had my share of desires and goals, but my life has come to me or I have gone to it mainly by way of mistakes and surprises. Often I have received better than I deserved. Often my fairest hopes have rested on bad mistakes. I am an ignorant pilgrim, crossing a dark valley. And yet for a long time, looking back, I have been unable to shake off the feeling that I have been led—make of that what you will [2000, p. 133].

I suspect that Jayber Crow's story is also a universal story; I know it is mine. I would love to have taken the King's Highway, but the path I have traveled has largely been unmarked, and I did not always know where I was going until I was there. The shortest distance home is a straight line, but that is not how I have traveled. I have circled and doubled back more times than I care to admit. I have experienced hell and purgatory and heaven but not in that sequence and not just once. I have cycled through them in different seasons and at different stages of my life. Often it is only in retrospect that I have understood the meaning of snares and toils I have encountered. I have been—and am being—shaped by my mistakes. I know I am a pilgrim. I suspect we all are.

Becoming True Self Is an Organic, Not Mechanistic, Process

There is a tendency to use a manufacturing metaphor—a mechanistic process—when thinking about how leaders, how all of us for that matter, grow and develop. It is a prevalent metaphor used in businesses (the right inputs lead to the right outputs), in schools (think of "No Child Left Behind"), in communities, and in religious organizations. The metaphor starts with the assumption that we can make everything— friends, money, meaning, even ourselves into the person we want to be. In *Finding Our Way* writer Margaret Wheatley says it this way: "In most of our endeavors—in science, health, and management—the focus is on creating better-functioning machines. We replace a faulty part, reengineer the organization, instill a new behavior or attitude, create a better fit, and recharge our batteries. The language and thinking is mechanistic" (2005, pp. 18, 19).

In a mechanistic process making a product is linear and sequential: follow the right steps in the right order and the result will be a good finished product. Furthermore, when the right quality control mechanisms are put into place, over time most if not all defects are eliminated. The process is called continuous improvement.

Not only do we want continuous improvement, but we also want speed and efficiency. Time-to-market is a critical variable to success. We think we must reduce product development time and manufacturing time so our company can get a "leg up" on its competition. In a similar way, companies keep looking for ways to shorten the time required to develop individuals into ideal leaders. If I need to become authentic to be effective, I will put it on my "to do" list for tomorrow.

This mechanical metaphor is used in many leadership development programs—including ones I have led—to help individuals identify strengths, eliminate or shore up weaknesses, and become better leaders. The thinking seems to be that if individuals identify and use their strengths, improve their weaknesses (minimize if not eliminate the defects), they can, over time, be made into something akin to ideal leaders. Another way of describing this process is that through a combination of the right genes, the right experiences and the ability to learn from them (the right inputs), certain individuals will evolve to a different level of being (the right output). This manufacturing metaphor and mechanistic theories assume that at the end of the process ideal leaders are produced, almost like producing the perfect widget.

Unfortunately, it simply does not work this way. "Individuals develop in their own time," write Morgan McCall and George Hollenbeck, "and processes, while not random, cannot be finely programmed nor predicted" (2010, p. 159). An authentic leader cannot be produced, even with the finest of mechanistic processes. And there is a cost when we try. When we think of ourselves as well-oiled machines we give up what it means to be real people. The prevailing assumption underlying some leadership development efforts that an individual can be made into an ideal leader is an illusion that does not serve us well. Sometimes we can and do construct a false self, a self we hope will be acceptable, but this self is a hollow self. Becoming the person we started out to be requires a different metaphor and a different process.

The best metaphor for describing the journey to true self is a natural one. Like nature, our lives are cyclical, not linear and sequential. The right inputs don't guarantee the right outputs; in fact, there are no guarantees, especially guarantees of continuous improvement. Our formation and development cannot be engineered.

Author Thomas Moore describes the reality of the soul's journey this way, "the soul doesn't evolve or grow. It cycles and twists, repeats and reprises, echoing ancient themes common to all human beings. It is always circling home" (2001). We humans are a living system. We live through different seasons, and then those seasons repeat themselves. In each season of our life there are experiences that shape and form us, that can help us recover our original shape.

Another important difference in these two metaphors is that the mechanical metaphor has a finished product while the nature metaphor does not. Becoming your true self and an authentic leader is not an end to be achieved. Instead, you and I are always in the process of becoming. At certain times we will find our way home and experience our self as whole and integral, and know what it means to lead as an authentic and true self. Then, as in the seasons, the cycle repeats itself, hopefully this time at a deeper level, a level where we have gotten past the illusion that our egocentric self is our true self, and have started grounding our self in the core of our being.

The simple but hard-to-fathom reality is that over the course of our lives we become our self again and again and again. I wonder if this isn't why Warren Bennis said we must "become the person we started out to be and enjoy the process of becoming." It is a process, not a destination, and it is better if we can enjoy the journey.

The Journey Need Not Be Taken Alone

The journey to true self is an intensely personal journey, and yet, the journey need not be taken alone. To stay the course, to find our way home to true self, to become an authentic leader, we need trustworthy traveling companions. Bill George and his colleagues have said, "Leaders cannot succeed on their own; even the most outwardly confident executives need support and advice. Without strong relationships to provide perspective, it is very easy to lose your way ... authentic leaders build extraordinary support teams to help them stay on course" (2007, p. 6).

Not every person we meet or work with is a good traveling companion on the journey; help is not always helpful. Under the guise of being helpful, others can add to our deformation in their attempts to set us straight. They steer us away from true self with their projections or expectations of who we ought to be.

At other times we find ourselves traveling with those who make no pretense of being helpful. The well-known Jewish theologian, Martin Buber, named and described "I-It" relationships, relationships that distort and deform true self. When we are used as a means to an end, used instrumentally, we are in an "I-It" relationship. When we are treated as an object we become an "It." When we are seen as simply a "human resource"—the name is interesting, isn't it?—we are an "It." When we find ourselves a pawn in a political game we know we are in an "I-It" relationship. When others attempt to fix or change us so we better meet their needs we are being treated instrumentally. When others try to shape or mold us so we will fit their preconceived notion of who we ought to be, we are in an "I-It" relationship. These are exactly the kind of relationships that will not be helpful on the journey toward true self.

Buber offers another option—the "I-Thou" relationship. Those who know how to create and maintain "I-Thou" relationships are the kind of people we want as traveling companions. In these relationships we are honored for who we are. Our true self, our soul, is respected as an end in and of itself, not as a means to an end. In an "I-Thou" relationship the other listens to us in ways that helps us discover or remember our self.

I-Thou relationships are similar to what Max DePree, former president of the highly respected furniture manufacturer Herman S. Miller, called covenantal relationships:

> Broadly speaking, there are two types of relationships in industry. The first and most easily understood is the contractual relationship. The contractual relationship covers the quid pro quo of working together ... [but] a contract has nothing to do with helping us reach our potential. Covenantal relationships, on the other hand, rest on shared commitments, to ideas, to values, to goals.... Words such as love, warmth, personal chemistry are certainly pertinent ... they fill deep needs and enable us to have meaning and to be fulfilling. Covenantal relationships reflect unity and grace and poise. They are an expression of the sacred nature of relationships [1989, p. 51].

In my own journey I have learned the importance of covenantal relationships. I know the importance of having friends, colleagues and bosses who are willing to listen deeply, ask questions that help me access the wisdom I have within me, be present with me while I find my true self, and who resist the temptation to give their well-meaning advice. I have learned the value of others who will help me stay on course by telling me the truth without judgment. I have learned how much I need others in my life with whom I can be completely and wholly myself. I have found that on my journey toward true self I need others who will respond to me as a "Thou" and will honor my essence, my soul, as an end in itself. These people are part of my "extraordinary support team."

An extraordinary support team can be a single individual, a group, or a network of individuals who are willing to walk beside us on the journey. The actual number of people is not as important as the nature of the relationship. In the work I do with the Center for Courage and Renewal, through programs like "Courage to Teach" and "Courage to Lead," we call the extraordinary support team a Circle of Trust. In these programs we carefully and intentionally create space in which true self feels safe to show up. In Circles of Trust individuals journey toward their true self in the company of good and helpful traveling companions.

The Journey Lasts a Lifetime

In one of her poems May Sarton says, "It takes time, many years and places" to become the person we started out to be (1993). There's no magic pill, no quick fix, no easy answers. We get bent out of shape time after time, and it takes a lifetime to recover our original shape. I once heard author Peter Koestenbaum say that we may never be totally true to ourselves, but making a commitment to move in that direction is important.

You and I are so used to maintaining a fast pace and believing in quick fixes (after all, on television shows life's thorniest problems are resolved in less than a half hour), the idea that the journey home takes a lifetime can be disquieting. Organizations want to turn out ideal leaders quickly. Shorten the workshop, speed up the learning process, and develop young high potentials in a hurry, as if the formation and development of people and leaders is another place to put efficiency experts to work. We live in a culture that loves fast food and express lanes; we call the mail system with which many of us grew up "snail mail." We step on the accelerator in every aspect of our life. We choose speed over depth in so many facets of our lives. But with patience and understanding, we can come to appreciate that the journey home takes time, and with this appreciation can decide not to rush the process, not to try to make it happen faster. There is no need to consider it one more thing to check off an already crowded "to do" list.

In *The Exquisite Risk*, poet and writer Mark Nepo describes the importance of welcoming the time it takes to become our self:

> If we don't take the time, we run the risk of arriving deformed. There is an old story of a man who came across a butterfly half-born from its

cocoon. It seemed to be struggling and so, trying to help, he gently exhaled his warm breath on it. Sure enough, his breath hastened its birth, but the butterfly fell to the ground, unable to fly. Its premature birth left its wings deformed. Our inward development can suffer the same fate, if we don't take the time to come full term.

Since speed and confidence are traits of success we are taught to strive with, it takes courage to welcome time and humility in our lives. Yet, without the openings that time and humility widen in us, the winds of life have no way to pass through and we stall our chance to become a true person [2005, p. 46].

Not only does it take a lifetime, but individuals don't usually turn toward home early in their life or career. Poet and essayist David Whyte suggests when we turn fifty is when we start returning home. Carl Jung had a similar understanding of how our life unfolds. Jung said we experience two distinct phases in life: the first he called "morning" and said that this was a time when we learn to relate to the outer world by developing our ego strength; the second he called "afternoon" and said that this was the time when we took an inner journey to reconnect with our true or real self (1960, para. 783).

When we actually turn the corner toward home is not important; the important point is that this is a universal story—you and I spend years in some guise other than our own. For me, it was beyond graduate school and the early years of my of my career—"many years"—before I began even asking the question of what it would mean for me to become the person I started out to be. The journey I am on in the "afternoon" of my life is very different than the journey I was on in the "morning."

The Journey Requires Contemplation

Given the fast-paced, consuming nature of work and leadership, staying the course, becoming the person we started out to be, requires the use of contemplative disciplines.

The first book I read by Parker J. Palmer was *The Active Life*. It is one of those books that I have been drawn back to at different times in my life. In the introduction Palmer suggests our contemporary images of what it means to contemplate are shaped by monastic metaphors—"silence, solitude, contemplation, and centeredness." The book title suggests another option: contemplation in the midst of an active life. Palmer says, "The purpose of contemplation in all its forms is to penetrate illusion and help us to touch reality" (1990, p. 25). Understood in this way, contemplation is not an option on the journey. Contemplative disciplines help us see that the face we sometimes wear is not our own. It is through contemplation that we realize the self we have carefully crafted is not our true self—it is an illusion we need to pierce. Through a contemplative discipline we can realize we are hiding rather than showing up, the values we espouse are not the ones we live, or we need courage in order to be true self.

Contemplation is not an option; it is also not easy. Palmer says it this way: "Contemplation is difficult for many of us because we have invested so much in illusion. Sometimes we even seem wedded to illusion as a way of survival." Because it is not easy, we often need crises or hardship experiences that disillusion us to get us started.

Different people will be drawn to different forms of contemplation. Some will prefer quieter disciplines like journaling, meditation or prayer, drawing, or writing poetry. Others will pierce their illusions in a more active life, while engaged in experiences like "chopping wood and carrying water," through I-Thou encounters, or though deep engagement in a community of faith. Whatever the form, the point is still the same: we need some form of contemplation if we are to become the person we started out to be.

Loving the Stranger Who Is Yourself

Poet Derek Wolcott wrote that when you return home "you will love again the stranger who was yourself ... the stranger who has loved you all your life, whom you ignored for another" (1986, p. 328). I wondered about this phrase for years. Who is the stranger who has loved me all of my life? Whom have I ignored for another?

Today my understanding is that the stranger is my whole and authentic self. The truth of my life, perhaps of yours also, is I have been so busy trying to be someone I am not—climbing ladders that others put in front of me, satisfying the needs of my ego, engaging in leadership out of a self I carefully crafted to please others—that I have ignored my authentic self. I have done it at my own peril. I have lost sight of the person I was created me to be. But my soul—my true self—has loved me all my life and is ready to greet me when I return home, when I arrive at my own door, when I reclaim what it means for me to be a whole and authentic human. This is for me the purpose of our personal journeys, our journey to becoming ourselves in our leadership roles, and our spiritual journeys—to become an authentic and whole person and leader.

4. Becoming and Being Authentic

Marcus is one of the lead characters in Michael Parker's latest novel, *All I Have in This World*. When he was a child Marcus tried to imagine what the legal charges meant that appeared in the local court docket— charges like check kiting and breaking and entering. When he was an adult Marcus kept remembering one of those charges, a "phrase that seemed to apply specifically to Marcus and that kept him up nights: *failure to appear*. How it terrified him, as all he wanted then and had wanted his whole life was the one thing he thought himself incapable of: to be present, to show up, and to participate" (2014, p. 210).

Failure to appear is a serious charge in our court system and in our leadership roles. It keeps us from engaging in the process of leadership as authentic men and women. Yet too often there is enough evidence to convict us of the charge. In the second chapter I offered some of the evidence:

- In leadership team meetings we say "yes" to a direction taken or decision made when we want to say "no"
- We do not speak our truth to others, especially those who have power over us, and then we blame them—after all, they do shoot the messenger, don't they?
- We hide our important beliefs and defining values when the heat is on or when our need to belong and be a team player is greater than our need to go public with our values
- We share data that supports our position rather than telling the whole truth; we hate spin and yet we spin the truth

- We wear someone else's face rather than our own
- We have more open and honest conversations in the parking lot after the meeting than we do during it

Like Marcus, we know what failure to appear means. And, like Marcus, one of the things we want—and have wanted our whole life—is to be present, to show up, and to participate.

Authenticity is one of the keys to leadership effectiveness. We want realness in the executive suite, in the superintendent's office, and in our religious leaders. We yearn for leaders who are themselves rather than a replica of someone else. We want leaders who will be fully human with us, men and women who are vulnerable enough to acknowledge their strengths and weaknesses, their gifts and limits, and who are appropriately transparent about their hopes and fears, their motivations and their agendas. We trust leaders who are real, who walk their talk, who act on their core values, and who tell us the truth. We authorize others to lead who author their own life. Those we deem not trustworthy we don't authorize to lead.

Authentic leadership is less about tips and techniques and toolkits and more about being, disclosing, and offering our true self. There is no best practice for doing this. Instead, it is understanding leadership as a state of being more than as a practice or a way of doing. It being who we are—being our true self—in particular and concrete leadership experiences.

There is also no quick fix. "It takes a lifetime to achieve authenticity," leadership theorist Peter Koestenbaum says (1991). As with becoming our true self, we are always more or less authentic. We are constantly in a process of being and becoming authentic. I have never gotten it all together in any kind of permanent way; I don't think any of us do. Instead, I become myself in the now, in a present moment, at a single point in time. I have been authentic self in one experience and found myself wearing someone else's face the next. I act with deep integrity in one meeting of a leadership team and sit mute in the next. I walk my talk some of the time, but not all of it. I have learned being authentic is not a destination but a quality of being we experience in particular times with particular people. During the course of my life and career I have had the opportunity to say many different times, "I was real and authentic in that experience." As I have learned from and been shaped by various experiences, I have been able to say this more and more of the time. I suspect the same is true of you. My hope is that as I learn and grow there will be more particular experiences where I can say I did not fail to appear.

Stories of Authenticity

I recently had the opportunity to observe a person act authentically—at least for a single experience—in a Courage to Lead retreat I facilitated. It was a retreat for a mixed group of professionals—educational leaders, community leaders, healthcare leaders, clergy leaders, and business leaders. The theme of the retreat was "Connecting Role and Soul"; the purpose was to provide participants a safe space to remember themselves, consider how to keep who they are connected with what they do, and think about what's required to show up in their leadership roles. After checking in and establishing some ground rules, participants were asked to reflect on those internal and external forces that encouraged them to show up and speak their truth. Then they were then invited to identify those forces that discouraged their true self from making an appearance, or worse, sent it into hiding.

To create a context for these questions I told a short version of the Abilene Paradox, a parable told by Jerry Harvey of a time when he and his wife's family went from Coleman, Texas, to Abilene for lunch on a sweltering August day and in a car without air conditioning, only to learn on the way home that no one had really wanted to go. Each had said yes to the trip because they thought other family members wanted to do it. Each had said yes when they wanted to say no. After a time of reflection on this story and during a time of sharing in the entire circle, one participant, who had been quiet throughout the morning, said, "I have lived in Abilene all my life. I haven't spoken my truth. I have said yes when I wanted to say no. I realized today that the only real force that keeps me in hiding is the fears and insecurities I carry inside me."

After the retreat I heard from this competent and caring clergy woman that she had returned to work that same day and told her boss she was going to quit hiding. Even at this initial meeting with her boss she showed up with all her fears and hopes, she was there in a whole-headed and whole-hearted way, and she spoke her truth. She was congruent and vulnerable—there was a match between her inner life and words she used. She told me later that they had one of their frankest, hardest, most open, and most productive conversations ever.

I have not heard from her since. I cannot tell you whether her resolve to come out of hiding and to stop going to "Abilene" lasted more than this one meeting. But I can tell you in that experience she was a whole and authentic person. Her soul and role were connected.

Several years ago I facilitated a team development experience for the executive team of a large nonprofit organization in the Midwest. There were seven members on the team, six had been on it for at least five years, and one was relatively new. The team was energized as they looked at their successes, both in terms of the outcomes they had achieved and the ways they had worked together, but the conversation took a decidedly different turn when they began to look at ways they could be more effective. Two individuals could have been accused of a failure to appear, others were more hesitant to speak up and when they did they used very tentative language, and one described the team's weakness so it sounded like strength. After a time one member of the team decided to name the elephant in the room, an elephant that everyone knew was there and had been there for some time, an elephant who might as well been named, "he who will not be discussed." This newest member of the team spoke his truth about the elephant without any blame or judgment. He simply and honestly described the behaviors he thought was hindering their team effectiveness. He acted with courage and authenticity. His courage was contagious; after he spoke others came out from hiding and shared their perspective on the elephant that now had a real name. Energy returned to individuals and the team. New possibilities emerged about what they might do together and hope grew for how they could work together in the future. Slowly and surely, but not easily, they became a stronger and more effective team.

Carla was the youngest and newest member of the senior management team of her large nonprofit organization, a team comprised mainly of older white males. I had the opportunity to observe her in action at the first planning retreat of the management team. One of the sensitive topics that surfaced was whether or not the senior managers would give themselves a year-end bonus, a bonus that would not be available to any other employees, and, if they did, if they would go public with it. After the briefest of conversations the team decided they would award themselves a bonus and they would keep it secret. There was one lone dissenting voice and it belonged to Carla. She appeared. She was open and honest and vulnerable. In a quiet but forceful way she made her case against the bonus and especially against any attempt to keep it secret. I remember how clearly she argued that these kinds of secrets undermine organizational effectiveness and create distrust. I was impressed.

On a recent Sunday I was worshipping at a large church in the city in which I live. The minister was starting a sermon series that was new and different for him—he was pushing his own envelope. When he started his sermon he said, "I may be out of my league here." I so appreciated his honesty from the pulpit that I trusted him and decided to journey with him into this uncharted water.

Stories of Inauthenticity

An executive looked at me in the middle of a one-on-one coaching session and said, "I have been told that outside of work I am warm and engaging, but that when I am at work I am a different person. I have a veneer that others find it difficult to get through. I don't know why I am this way. But I don't like it, and I know from experience that when others are not genuine or real it is harder for me to trust them. One of the reasons I asked for a coach is to help me figure out how I can be the same person at work as I am outside of it."

At the start of a team building experience with a new team of executives, formed by the merging of two existing divisions, I asked those present to suggest and then agree to norms on how they would function together during the several days we would be together. After a few other rules for the road were suggested one member said, "I want us to agree to turn our cards over face up. It is only going to work if we are honest." All other team members agreed to this being a norm. At the end of the first session and before we went to lunch I asked the team members to reflect on our process vis-à-vis the agreed upon norms. To a person they agreed they were paying attention to the norms, and in particular they commented on how honest everyone was being. I stopped in the men's restroom to wash my hands before eating, and two of the executives followed me in. As they were entering, one said to the other, "Russ is really naïve if he thinks we are going to tell the truth in this setting."

I served on the board of a small organization for several years, and one of the disturbing things I noticed is that the board members found it easy to talk about the executive director but hard if not impossible to talk with him. This truth came home to me when it was time for the director's annual review; things that were said before the review about the director were not said to him during the review.

I facilitated a week-long workshop at the Center for Creative Leadership. In the introductions on the first day a senior level manager in a large organization said, "My boss always says to me that I should not let the real me come out, that I should be the person I need to be to get the job done." For this boss, failure to appear was a necessary requirement. I was astonished. Listen again to his message: don't be real. Put on the game face necessary for the situation. Be whoever you need to be to get the job done.

The workshop I was facilitating that week featured a realistic simulation called Looking Glass, Inc. (LGI), developed at the Center for Creative Leadership. Over the years I have watched hundreds of managers spend a day as the executive leadership team of this simulated company. Time after time these managers and executives have demonstrated how hard it is for all of us to show up and be authentic. One of the sticky, political problems built into this simulation is Project Deepsea, a costly research and development project intended to develop an underwater glass for use in submarines. The participants in the simulation need to decide whether or not to continue the R&D funding. They know there is no evidence in any memo or e-mail that LGI can build the glass to the Navy's specifications, and no commitment from the Navy to buy the glass if it is developed. They also know the company has poured too many product development dollars into it.

As one participant said after the simulation, "Looking Glass should deep-six deepsea." But it is seldom done—the last time I saw the data it was about 20 percent of the time. The reason: there is one memo in the simulation calling Project Deepsea the president's "pet project." This is what makes it sticky. No one wants to tell the president it should be deep-sixed. What I find remarkable is that this holds true even though this is just a simulation and there are no real consequences if the messenger does get shot. The participants in the simulation are usually mid- to senior level managers from Fortune 1,000 companies—even seasoned managers, not just less experienced ones, find it hard to show up and speak the truth. They, too, can be cited for failure to appear. It is hard to be authentic. It is easier, and appears safer, to ignore certain problems or hope someone else will handle them, even if it means pouring product development dollars down a rat hole.

Learning to Be Inauthentic

We learn to be inauthentic. Others teach, but we learn, and we learn the lessons well. Throughout our lives and careers we taught that the failure to appear is safe and sane, sometimes the wise thing to do, that at times it is better to not show up, better to hide our deepest values and beliefs, better to not speak the truth. We are taught this through the process of socialization.

Early in life parents and parent-figures (teachers, aunts and uncles, older siblings) have rules, shoulds and oughts, and expectations and standards that they use to teach us about right and wrong ways to be and do. Given their knowledge and resources, they do the best they can to help us become responsible adults. We trust their intent—their motive is to be helpful; they do not mean to teach us to be inauthentic, but rather they want to contribute to our "peoplemaking."

Peoplemaking is one of the favorite books I read during graduate school and the author, Virginia Satir, was one of my best teachers. In *Peoplemaking*, Satir wrote about the rules that exist in families, rules that dictated what children should see and hear, what they should feel and think, what they should say. Satir called these rules the "Unfreedoms." I remember the same rules in my family: "If you can't say something nice don't say anything at all." "Do not talk back to me" (or to any authority figures, like teachers or scout leaders); my mother said at least a million times, "don't be impudent." I did not know the meaning of the word, but I got the message from the tone of her voice. "Don't ever say you hate anyone." "Don't be angry with your sister." And along with all these there was, ironically, another message: "Always be honest."

4. *Becoming and Being Authentic*

I assume you can remember some of the "shoulds" and "oughts" you learned in your childhood. One reason we move in and out of being authentic as adults is because of these "unfreedoms" we learned while growing up. Early childhood experiences form and deform us.

These parental expectations and standards for the right way to be and do were then reinforced by some of our teachers in school. My second grade teacher, to name but one example, really did want me to sit down, shut up, and color in the lines, and she clearly thought fear was the way to get me to do it. If I did not do what she said, I would be sent to the hall to wait for the principal to come by with his "board of education." With this principal there was no due process; it was "bend over, grab you ankles" and take a swat. A little later I had an eighth grade football coach who would send us to the "shoe factory" if we did not do what he expected. Translated, he would plant his foot on our backside to remind us he meant business.

Work experiences contribute to our socialization. One of the first bosses I had in corporate America had a clear way of creating one-up, one-down relationships, and I and his other subordinates were reminded often that we were just that: subordinate to him. I have known and worked with another boss who really did "shoot the messenger," and another who asked for feedback and said they valued it but who got angry and defensive when it was offered. I have heard first person stories of bosses who ridicule employees in public, who use their intelligence to make other people feel stupid, who "slice and dice" employees, or who "cut them off at the knees" when they suggest a "stupid" idea. With these bosses, failure to appear behavior appears to be the smart thing to do; the seemingly rational response is to go into hiding,

Even the organizations for which we work have informal norms that let us know the right ways to be and do. Over time, we slowly adapt. We change our way of being and doing to fit the organizational expectations. I know of one organization that describes itself as a "gentleman's club"—all conflict, including conflict in the executive suite, remains under the surface. Politeness and respect are core values. Those who work in this organization learn that politeness, not confrontation, is the expected behavior. I know of another company that says it prizes open and honest communication, including giving feedback up and down the hierarchy, but giving honest feedback is not the norm inside the company, and individuals working there conform their behavior to fit what's expected.

To be sure, there are many ways that parents, teachers, coaches, scout leaders, bosses and others help who shape and form us, encourage us to become and be our true self, the person we started out to be. They name our gifts and help us discern our limits. They help us learn the right lessons from our successes and our failures. They provide a safe and trustworthy environment for us to try on different guises as we seek to discover our own true face. They are among those we think of as trustworthy traveling companions.

But the point still remains that there are many experiences with others that leave us bent us out of shape and deformed, that encourage us to feed our false-self system. We learn that there are acceptable ways to be and do, and sometimes learn that being inauthentic is what is acceptable. We show up as the person others expect us to be rather than whom we are, as false self rather than true self. We decide there are some thoughts and feelings we should not express. We learn it is not safe to challenge some authority figures. We hide or spin the truth; we do not act on our core values; we say "yes" to decisions being made or directions being taken when we want to say "no." Thus begins the divide between our inner life and outer work.

It would be healthy and life-giving for us and good for the organizations we serve if we grew out of this tendency to hide as we grow older, if we were authentic more and more of the time as we matured. Some do. Some people who are "long of tooth," who are in the afternoon of life, sometimes feel freer to be authentic and tell the truth. Others, even those in the morning of life, have taken the journey home to true self and have made a clear and conscious decision to stay true more of the time. Yet others find living a divided life is so painful that they choose, even at great risk, to be authentic.

But some don't. Though we move in and out of being authentic, there are some who remain guilty of failure to appear far too much of the time. Cultural anthropologist Angeles Arrien says that we continue to hide "by editing our thoughts, rehearsing our emotions, performing what we think other people want to see, or hiding our true selves. We feed the false-self system whenever are unwilling to tell the truth, say what is so, or give voice to what we see" (1993, p. 94). The problem of being authentic continues as long as we think our false self is our real and authentic self and think of it as our objective reality.

Courage Is Required

I have said it before, but it bears repeating: it takes courage to be our authentic and true self. Courage is required to act on our deepest values and beliefs. It takes courage to live and lead as whole-headed and whole-hearted men and women. It takes courage to take off our game face and wear our own. But unfortunately, there are no skills that empower us to show up as true self, state our positions on important issues clearly and honestly, walk our talk when the heat is on, to say "no" when we mean "no." In fact, there is nothing "out there"—no tips or techniques that can provide us the courage we need. Instead, courage comes from within; it comes when our leadership is grounded in our true self. It comes when we assume responsibility for authoring our own lives. It comes when being authentic is more important than being safe and secure.

One of the first tasks I was assigned when I joined the human resource staff of a major oil and gas company was to develop a training program to teach managers and executives the skills needed to give helpful feedback both during annual performance reviews and during day-to-day work. The president of the company believed that all men and women deserved to know how they were doing. He was right but it wasn't happening. The company had data showing only a small percentage of employees were getting any performance appraisal, much less helpful ones. My own first performance appraisal, for example, was done in the way of the office on a Friday afternoon when my boss handed me a sheet showing my merit increase and thanked me for doing a good job—and this was in the human resources group.

The shared belief in this company was that individual managers were not giving performance appraisals because they did not know how. It was a lack of skill, not will, or so I and others thought. We believed there was something out there—in this case, a particular set of skills in giving feedback and handling defensive responses—that would enable managers and executives to provide employees the feedback they wanted and deserved. We spent countless hours designing and delivering a performance appraisal skills training program. Most managers and executives participated. As workshops go, the program was a good one. It was experiential education at its best—some lecture, but mostly behavior modeling and skill practice.

After several years we stopped the training program long enough to assess the results of our efforts. We collected reams of data, from past workshop participants and from employees who reported to those participants. To put it simply, we learned what we were doing was not working. We learned that helping managers develop new skills was important but not sufficient. After hours of skill practice, managers remained reluctant to give feedback and, when they did it wasn't usually honest or helpful. We learned that the problem was not lack of skill; it was a lack of courage. There wasn't something "out there"—no tools to add to the toolkit—that could be acquired to enable managers to give honest and open feedback; managers and the rest of us fail to give feedback because of something "in here." That something "in here" ranges from fear to insecurity to a need for affection and approval from others.

I was surprised by our finding. I assumed managers in corporate America were tough and strong, that sitting across the table and giving someone feedback would be a proverbial walk in the park. I thought they would show up at performance appraisal time, be real and honest, speak the truth to the person, and be congruent and transparent. I was wrong. These managers could have been cited for failure to appear.

The early work experience I had in this oil and gas company has been reinforced in many other experiences. The workshops I facilitate at the Center for Creative Leadership are feedback-intensive. Participants are offered a helpful and constructive process for giving feedback to each other; we call it Situation-Behavior-Impact, or S-B-I.

S-B-I is a simple, helpful, and elegant way of giving feedback. It begins with locating the feedback in a time and place, the situations: "In the meeting this morning" ... "As we were walking to lunch and I was telling you about the trouble I was having with an employee...." Then a very specific behavior is described, and described without evaluation or interpretation: "You pointed out what data in my report had been especially helpful to you as you prepared one for our boss" ... "you interrupted me and said, 'put on your big boy pants.'" Finally, the impact of the behavior is described: "I was proud that I had made a contribution to the final report" … "I felt demeaned." Participants understand the model, are allowed opportunities to practice using it, and most seem to get it. But actually giving feedback to others, especially developmental feedback, is hard to do. Even the idea of doing it causes anxiety and resistance.

This same dynamic was at work in the senior management team of the company who said they "wanted to turn the card over face up" but then did not do it. It was evident in the nonprofit organization which board members talked about the executive director but not to him, and in the church where the clergy leader talks to others about his conflict with the choir director rather than to her. It is the same reality that causes us to go to Abilene, to say "yes" when we want to say "no." And it is the same root problem that caused a senior executive of a large university to tell me recently that she assigned a "mediocre" employee less meaningful work in hopes he would get bored and decide to leave the organization.

The problem in each of these situations is not that the manager or executive lacked skill or will. The problem was a lack of courage. Courage is always required for us to be authentic. It is often the missing ingredient.

Developing Courage

I have long pondered the source of courage. The question I have asked over and over is "where do you and I get the courage that is required to come out of hiding and be our authentic and true self?" There is no college or university course that can teach us the courage we need. I know of no leadership development experience that has as an expected outcome the learning of courage.

Instead, we learn by doing, by being true and acting on what we believe. We develop courage every time we make a decision to be and stay true and we learn from these experiences that being authentic is freeing and life-giving. In single experiences we decide not to trade our integrity for safety and security, and we like ourselves better; we feel more whole and authentic. And we learn our fears are often unfounded, that very seldom do they actually shoot the messenger. Conversely, we learn from other experiences, from the times we decide to stay in hiding, what it is like to add to our own diminishment as a person.

At other times we find our courage only when the pain of being our false self becomes too great. We realize wearing a game face, not speaking the truth, or hiding our most precious values is slowly tearing at the fabric of our identity. We do not like who we are or what we are doing. We know at some deep level who we are is disconnected from what we do and we do not like it.

While there is no tip or technique—nothing "out there"—that can teach us courage, others can help. Over and over again, in one setting or another, I have seen one act of courage spawn another. Courage is contagious. One person is vulnerable, transparent, and authentic in a meeting of consequence and others decide to be and do likewise.

Courage comes from others in another way. Trustworthy traveling companions can encourage us. This is different than empowering us; this phrase, widely-used and now part of our lexicon, suggests that power is a currency that can be given or taken away, rather than as something rooted in our true self. Waiting to be empowered to be authentic in the process of leadership is akin to waiting for Santa Claus to come. But others can provide necessary support. They can listen to us in ways that help us work through our fears and anxieties and find our own voice. They can reinforce us when we show up. Ron Heifetz and Marty Linsky call these trustworthy traveling companions "confidants." "They provide you with a place where you can say everything that's in your heart, everything that's on your mind, without being predigested or well-packaged ... they can remind you why it is important to get out there and takes risks in the first place ... confidants must be willing to tell you what you do not want to hear and cannot hear from anyone else" [2002, pp. 199–200].

But even when others display courage or encourage us, courage finally comes from within us. It is rooted in our wholeness and authenticity. We find courage deep within us and act authentically, and when we act authentically we develop our courage.

The Risks and Rewards of Being Authentic

Even with courage and the right skills, we can minimize but never eliminate the risks that come with being authentic. When we choose to be real, to be vulnerable, we open ourselves up to others in ways that are risky. One clear piece of evidence that showing up and speaking the truth is risky is how most organizations now have in place rules and regulations to protect "whistleblowers" who dare to speak the truth. Our understandable desire is to shield ourselves from these risks. In *Leadership on the Line*, Ron Heifetz and Marty Linsky say it this way: "In our work with men and women all over the world, in all walks of life, we have seen good people take on the cloak of self-protection to insulate themselves from the dangers of stepping out. Self-protection makes sense; the dangers are real" (2002, p. 225).

Because of these dangers I have struggled with being authentic—and the related notions of being honest and real and vulnerable—most of my life. I have especially struggled with speaking the truth to those who have had power over me, those who could reward or punish me. With them I too often found it easier to say what I thought they wanted to hear, put a particular spin on the truth, or not tell the whole story. The risk of doing otherwise seemed too great.

Sometimes the risks are too great, the dangers are real, and it is truly not safe to be honest and authentic. There are punitive bosses, powerful lay leaders in a religious organization, or executive directors of nonprofit organizations who really do kill the messenger, or at least respond with over-the-top anger and hostility. Being transparent and vulnerable at these times seems unwise, and we decide that staying in hiding is reasonable and rational.

At other times we decide there is no realistic prospect for a positive outcome from being real or honest and so we decide not to appear, or we appear only briefly. The decision made to go to Abilene, or some version of it, is firm and final, and our opinion will not matter. In a decision-making process our input is not sought, our dissenting view is not heard, and we return to a safe hiding place. When the Looking Glass president is determined to proceed with Project Deepsea, when the school district seems committed to a new reading program without the input or shared agreement of teachers (having direction without alignment is all too common in leadership processes), and when the clergy leader is determined to change the order of worship regardless of our views because he has the "authority" to do so, we can easily justify our decision not to appear.

My struggle is to know the difference between those times I fail to appear because there is a real reason to fear, or there is no possible positive payoff, and when I don't show up because of my own internal anxieties and insecurities. I confess that too often it is what is going on "in here," not someone or something "out there," that keeps me from speaking the truth. At these times I make a dangerous exchange: I swap my authenticity for what appears to be safety and security.

Over the course of my career and life I have slowly learned the risks of being transparent and authentic cut both ways. There is a danger in putting it all on the line, of showing up in our own face, of speaking the truth. But there is also a risk to hiding or to showing up with our game face on. We hide our most important beliefs and values, we tell others what they want to hear rather than the truth, we agree to a direction planned when we know it will take the organization in the wrong way, and in the process we gradually tear at the fabric of our identity. We lose parts of ourselves. Our interactions with others are more death-giving than life-giving. Slowly but surely we become less whole, more fragmented.

Learning to Speak the Truth in Helpful Ways

Courage is often the missing ingredient, but along with courage we also need the right skill. Skill does matter. How we show up—the language we use, the tone of our voice, the body language we exhibit—is important.

I learned this lesson from hard experiences, some my own, some from others. I learned, for example, that when some people ask to give me constructive criticism and I say yes, I may have given them permission to judge, blame and criticize. Too often I am evaluated rather than given knowledge about a behavior they want me to stop or start doing. I do not get helpful feedback. And here's the kicker: because I gave them permission my fingerprints are on their knife.

I have seen managers and executives who, under the pretense of being honest, denigrate and demoralize people who work for them; they "tell the truth" but do it in a way that sucks the life and energy out of the very people they must rely on to do important work well. I have observed senior executives dismiss ideas crudely and cruelly—"hand them [a subordinate] their head on a platter." I have heard a clergy leader label a staff member as "stuck in her ways" and "living in the past," rather than speak the truth to her with language that described an unacceptable behavior.

No matter how honest we think we are being, when we send messages that blame or judge, that tell others what they should or ought to do, that moralize or label, that threaten, that evaluate, or that are designed to "fix" the other, it makes matters worse, never better. They create more defensiveness and resistance than buy-in and change. If our goal is to influence anything, from a decision or vision for the organization to encouraging another person to stop or start a behavior, we need to learn more helpful ways of speaking the truth.

Here's a key I learned from the writing of Angles Arrien: we need to learn to speak the truth without blame or judgment. Or as one colleague from CCL once put it, we need to be 100 percent honest and 100 percent kind. These are skills that can be learned. Though skill training is not the focus of this book, we can learn to send "I-Messages," or use CCL's S-B-I feedback model to develop the skills we need to speak the truth without blame or judgment.

Staying True

There are at least three things you and I must do if we are to stay true to ourselves and be authentic more and more of the time.

Manage our fears and interpersonal needs. To repeat what I confessed earlier, more often than not it is my fears and anxieties that keep in hiding more than any realistic assessment of how the other might respond. It is what is going on in my inner life, not anything going on in the outer world, which keeps me tied up in knots. This has particularly been true throughout my career as I anticipated speaking truth to power. I know that my fears and anxieties keep me in hiding: I suspect the same is true for many of you. In order to be authentic, I need to manage these fears.

I also need to manage my interpersonal needs. Early in my career I learned that I have a high need for inclusion and affection (the need to be liked and appreciated) and these needs drive my behavior. When

I think that if I speak my truth you may not like me, or worse, withhold your affection from me, I may choose to stay in hiding. These interpersonal needs influence my behavior, but they do not determine it. I can and do manage these needs and so can you. I can and do consciously choose to be authentic even at the risk of a particular person not meeting these needs; you can do likewise.

Maintain strong relationships with trustworthy traveling companions. I have already written about the importance of others, of confidants, in this chapter, but the idea is important and deserves to be emphasized. The journey to authenticity and wholeness is not one we can, or need, to take alone. It does not matter if we call these people trustworthy traveling companions, confidants, or true friends, the important point is that we need others who will walk beside us on our journey home to true self and authentic leadership. We move in and out of being authentic, of being at home and then getting lost again, and trustworthy traveling companions can help us find our way back to our self when we lose sight of who we are. They do this not by fixing us, but by listening to us, by encouraging us, and by shining a light in the darkness. They allow us to try on different guises as we seek to find our own true face, and they do it without judgment of any kind. And, as Heifetz and Linsky suggested, they tell us what is hard for us to hear, and they do it with great love.

Find experiences and places that renew. It is a busy and stress-filled world in which we live, a world in which we can easily become dismembered or pulled apart. We need time and opportunities to re-member ourselves; experiences that allow us to get in touch again with the true self that resides at the center of our being. Sadly, given the fast-paced, 24/7 world in which we live, these are the places and experiences we often give up first. We tell ourselves that we simply do not have time for reflection and renewal. But my experiences suggest just the opposite is true: the "hurrieder" we go, the more we need time for re-creation and renewal.

For me, the place I go to for reflection and renewal is the cabin my wife and I own in the mountains of western North Carolina. We named it *Temenos,* which means quiet place, or sanctuary place, and it is that for me. The setting invites contemplation. I go there and re-member myself. I get in touch again with my true self or soul, and consider what it means for me to stay true and be authentic.

For you the place or experience may be different. For some of our friends the place is the beach rather than the mountains. For an educational leader I know the place is New York City and the experiences include seeing plays, eating really good food, and sleeping long hours. For a clergy leader with whom I have worked one experience that is renewing is long-distance running. For a colleague at the Center for Creative Leadership it is being on a sail boat. For a business leader it is travel to distant places, places where she gets different perspectives on life and work. Different places and experiences but the same purpose: time to stop-look-listen, to catch our breath, to remember who we are on the other side of false self and ego self, and to be renewed.

5. Becoming and Being
a Whole Person

A conversation with a seasoned executive took a strange turn, at least strange to me. "There are so many competing demands and pressures at work that I am feeling pulled apart—the image I have in my head is that different people have ropes tied around my waist and each is pulling me in a different direction. And I am so concerned about what is going on in the company that I don't sleep well at night—the strategy we adopted is not working, last quarter's results were dismal, employee morale is in the tank—and yet at work I try to keep an optimistic upbeat attitude. And some days I think that I do not have the gifts and skills and energies needed to do the job. There has got to be a better way to be and do leadership. But what is it? What do I need to do differently?"

I understand his questions. After experiences leave us dissolved and shaken, we yearn to experience ourselves as integrated. After experiences leave us bent if not broken, we want to be restored. After feeling pulled apart, being dismembered, by competing demands and expectations at work, we want to re-member ourselves and be whole again. But the questions "what is it?" and "what do I need to do differently?" are hard to answer.

There is no clear path or simple recipe for this executive to follow. But I suggest that there are four things that he—and we—must integrate on our journey toward wholeness: inner life and outer work, light and shadow, gifts and limits, and our various energies—mental, physical, emotional, and spiritual. Over the course of my life and from many different leadership experiences I have learned that these are crucial parts of our life that must be fused and made indissoluble for the executive—or you or me—to say "I was myself in that leadership experience."

For years I thought that if I had courage and did the hard work of integration I would arrive at a destination, an end point. I thought that after wandering in the wilderness, I would, like the ancient Israelites, arrive in a promised land and stay there. I thought that was the point: to arrive. I believed that if I focused on identifying and honing my strengths, polishing and using my gifts, and improving my weaknesses, I would keep getting better and better until I became the idealized person I presented myself as being. I just knew that somehow and sometime I would "get it all together." And when I arrived I would be whole or integrated, always able to experience life and engage in leadership as a whole person

But this is not how my life has unfolded. Arriving and staying put have not been part of my experience. I realized along the way that I always have to pay attention to my being and my doing. I could not take my eye off the road. If I did, I would wind up in a ditch of my own making. I would revert and disown my gifts, deny my shadow, or disregard the impact of my inner life on my outer work.

A word of caution: slippery roads lie ahead. Integrating the various parts of our self into a whole person is not the stuff of any academic program on leadership, or of most leadership development programs. Most of these programs focus on the so-called "hard stuff" of leading. The inner work of leadership is considered the "soft stuff." But take the journey toward becoming a whole self and you will discover that the soft stuff is the hard stuff. The work of integration and becoming whole is not for the faint of heart.

Fusing Inner Life and Outer Work

Good to Great is one of my favorite books of recent years. Its author James Collins calls the type of leadership required to turn a good organization into a great one "Level 5 leadership." Collins argues that companies are able to move from good to great when there is an "inner development of a person to Level 5" leadership (p. 37).

We don't often pay attention to inner development. Of all the "soft stuff" executives and managers—and all the rest of us, for that matter—try to avoid, inner life issues and inner development may appear the softest of all. What goes on inside us cannot be studied empirically; it cannot be quantified. The correlation to any bottom line measure cannot be easily made. Inner life, and its interplay with outer work, has not been part of the curriculum of any formal education course, and only a few of the many leader development programs I have led or know about.

Instead, leader development courses of all types tend to focus on teaching the knowledge, skills, and competencies individuals need to effectively navigate the permanent whitewater that exists within the organization and in the external environment in which the organization exists and seeks to thrive. Learning to live and succeed in the external world is tough enough; it takes focus and skill and lots of effort to pull off. And, as suggested earlier, we tend to look outside of our self for techniques, comfortable formulas, or clues to help us do it.

For many years, including years I was managing and leading people, I looked outside of myself for clues that would enable me to be more effective. In the language of the Myers-Briggs Type Indicator (MBTI), an instrument that helps identify personality preferences, I am an ESTJ, or Extraverted Sensing Thinking Judging person (as soon as I write this I want to remind myself, and you, that there is a real person on the other side of these four letters). But the meaning behind these four letters suggests something about my personality type, something about my nature, my human nature, and something about my gifts and limits. Among other things is says that my preference is to take cues from the external world, from people and events outside of me. I do not have a natural tendency to pay attention to inner life issues. But these Myers-Briggs preferences do not *determine* me or my behavior; I can and do act in ways that are out-of-preference. Slowly and over time, and with the help of trusted friends, I have learned to pay attention to what is going on in my inner life. What I have learned is that what goes on in my inner world affects who I am and what I do in the outer world and, conversely, that what goes on in the external world affects what I experience internally. There is no way for me to de-couple or split the two.

One of the most helpful mirrors held up to me so I could see the relationship of my inner life and outer work more clearly is the FIRO-B (Fundamental Interpersonal Relationship Orientation-Behavior). Will

Schutz developed the FIRO-B to assess three dimensions of interpersonal needs—the need for inclusion, control, and affection. I have taken the instrument a number of times through the years and my results are always close to the same: I have a high need for inclusion, a moderate need to control (have impact, influence, to give direction), a very low threshold for being controlled, and a high need for affection (that is, want others to express openness and warmth toward me, and I need to do the same toward them).

Nothing is wrong with these scores; they don't point to any pathology. But I have learned that my inner need for inclusion and affection impact my leadership behaviors, and my leadership behaviors affect my inner life. Because of my high need for affection—a need for you to express warmth and appreciation toward me—I am careful about how I give direction, how I confront, and how I engage in conflict. I do not want to risk that you will withhold your appreciation or affection. At the same time, what happens in my relationships can affect my internal feelings about myself—for example, when I am feeling included and affirmed I am more likely to speak my truth. Inner life and outer work are inextricably linked; they are fused, cleanly or poorly, in our life and our leadership roles.

For a long time I thought I could manage these needs and keep them from impacting my engagement in leadership. Now I know this is not true. For me, part of "fusing"—and a way to keep relationships clean, not messy—is to acknowledge and embrace these preferences and interpersonal needs, and be aware of the interplay between them and my outer work. What I now know is that when I deny or try to ignore my need for affection or approval those needs tighten their grip on me. But when I acknowledge that they are part of me, that I am whole because of them not in spite of them, they lose part of their sway over me.

Sid Batts is one of my favorite people. He is the senior pastor at First Presbyterian Church in Greensboro, North Carolina, a keen observer of people, and a student of leadership. Several years ago I was in a team development experience with Sid and we were talking about what we had learned over time about leadership. At one point he said something like, "the truth is that if we are a mess on the inside we will be a mess on the outside," including, I add, in our engagement in leadership. This is not just my story; it is a human story; it is the story the leaders with whom I have worked over the years and whom I have come to know, in workshop settings or in one-to-one relationships. Here are but three examples:

- The president of a medium-sized and well-known organization was truly a mess on the inside. She had such a high need for inclusion and control that she gave direction when it was not needed, wanted most if not all decisions to be pushed up to her (or else she would pull them up), did not delegate easily and never fully turned loose of the management reins. In her own words, she wanted to be "respected more than I need to be liked." What she did not see is how her need for control left others feeling disempowered and dispirited, and fostered compliance but not commitment. She was neither liked nor respected.
- The president of a well-known organization had such a strong desire to please others, accompanied by a strong need to be liked, that, without meaning to or being fully aware of doing so, he tended to side with the last person in his office. This behavior sent a lot of different messages in the organization about what he wanted. For this person, like for many of us, there were occasions when inner life and outer work were not fused. This president was not just a mess on the inside; he created a mess on the outside.
- The senior pastor of a "high steeple" church who had a high need for control *and* a belief that he—and others—should be servant leaders. He honestly thought he could keep his need for control repressed; he worked hard to do so. But the result was as inevitable as it was clear: he continually said one thing about the best way to lead—as a servant—but led another way. He did not walk his talk. He was the proverbial wolf in sheep's clothing.

But these are not the only kind of stories out there. There are stories of men and women who fuse inner life and outer work, to wit:

- A director in a large corporation knew that his need for affection and appreciation and approval drove many of his decisions, including his decision not to give honest feedback when it was needed, but he was open and transparent about this need, and was intentional about staying present when differences or conflict arose.

- A young woman, identified in her organization as someone with high potential, knew that she had a lot of insecurity and anxiety in her shadow, and her worst fear was that others would see her as the imposter she thought of herself as being. She was intentional about taking the hard journey down and in to name and embrace her shadow, and so when she became a vice president in the organization she knew what she needed to do to avoid projecting her shadow onto others and thus create dark, shadowy places where they had to work.

- The pastor of a large membership church acknowledged both his gifts and his limits, and made sure the staff and lay leaders of the congregation knew about both. The pastor also made sure others had strengths that complemented his own, and in the language of Max DePree, he "abandoned himself to the strengths of others." As this pastor acknowledged his gifts and limits, his strengths and weaknesses, he gained personal power and influence. He became a trusted leader.

These are not stories of these individuals alone. They are like "everyman" morality plays—they are stories of each of us. They are stories that give us hope—hope that on our journey we will continue to learn from the constant and inevitable interplay between our inner life and outer work.

Fusing Light and Shadow

Let's go deeper. There is one inner life/outer work reality that has an enormous and often unrecognized impact on our practice of leadership. All of us cast light and shadow. It is not a choice, and none of us are exempt. But when we are engaged in accomplishing leadership tasks we cast light and shadow in a way that literally and metaphorically helps others find light or keeps them in the dark.

As I mentioned in the last chapter, I developed an intellectual understanding of shadow from the writing of Carl Jung, and his description of the difference in our persona, the self we show in public, and our shadow, that part of ourselves we try to hide. Jung wrote, "Everyone carries a shadow and the less it is embodied in a person's conscious life, the blacker and denser it is" (Jacobi 1973, p. 133). In this single sentence Jung points to two critical realities: each of us has a shadow side and, as much as we might wish it were not true, our shadow is part and parcel of our identity. The more we deny this truth, the less we acknowledge and "own" our shadow, the denser and blacker it becomes.

I knew about the concept of the shadow from reading Jung and others, but for a long time I kept it at arm's length. It was not until the experience of a divorce and the counseling I went through at the time that I had a live encounter with the "strangers" that dwell within me. When I first really understood—understood not just in my head but deep down in my gut -that I carried a shadow within me, I thought of it as a foreigner, a stranger within, and I wanted to rid myself of it as quickly as possible. It was nigh impossible for me to imagine that my shadow had any useful function, that it had served me well in life or leadership. Certainly, I did not see it as part of my nature, my identity. If I had a shadow, it had to be an intruder from the outside whom I would quickly show to the door. Or so I thought.

The therapist with whom I worked during this time was a good companion for this leg of my journey. It was in this safe trustworthy relationship that I was able, for the first time, to acknowledge that I was full of insecurities and anxieties. I was also able to understand, again for the first time, how often my shadow was projected onto personal and professional relationships. What I learned is that my shadow does not stay buried—it pops out to haunt me and hurt others, and does so at all the wrong times. One example: I remember a specific time when I was directing the work of an important group at CCL and was feeling insecure about the right strategic direction for us to go in order to continue to grow the business. My doubt and insecurity surfaced as anger—this helped no one, and it hurt everyone.

With the therapist's firm gentle support, I began the process of accepting and then making my peace with these "monsters" that dwelled within. I still remember the day she asked me to consider dancing with my shadow rather than trying to get rid of it. Dancing was an interesting

phrase for her to use. How, I wondered, would I ask it to dan
would I hold it? Do I want a slow dance or a fast one? Should I take uic
lead or let it? I decided to approach my shadow gently but firmly, that
a slow dance would be the right place to start, and that I would hold it
rather loosely.

What I learned, and am learning, is that my shadow is part of me,
that in important ways it has served me well, and that I need to befriend
and integrate it, not rid myself of it. I also learned that it takes courage
to acknowledge and then integrate my shadow. I like the idea that I can
and do cast light into the dark corners of the world, and I am pleased
when others think I do. But I don't like the idea of casting shadow, especially projecting my shadow onto others in ways that create dark places
for them to live and work. I particularly don't like the idea of casting a
shadow when I am engaged in leadership. But I do—and all my experiences say I am not alone in doing this. Just as a tall building casts a
longer shadow so those engaged in accomplishing leadership tasks cast
longer shadows. For this reason, it is critical that leaders take the courage
to look in the mirror, see what's actually there, and fuse it.

One problem is that too many of us engaged in leadership tasks
know little about our shadow and the way it impacts our leadership
behavior. In today's parlance, we simply "don't want to go there." As suggested before, many activities of leadership focus on the externals—on
envisioning the future, on making critical strategic decisions, on building
and maintaining alignment, and on producing lasting and useful change.
It is tough enough to wrestle with these tasks; there is no need, the thinking seems to be, to go on an inward journey to identify parts of ourselves
we wish weren't there.

But our shadow is part of our selves, and it does matter. Let me
share several brief stories to illustrate how shadow matters in leadership
activities:

- Gene was a senior executive—the leader at the top—of several
  organizations when I met him. He enjoyed successes and
  suffered failures. The success he deserved. He possessed a
  towering intellect, had courage enough to face even the most
  difficult of challenges, and could be warm and charming. His
  failures were also deserved. He was an anger-based person. He

could turn from warm and charming to angry in a split
second. When he did so, he used his intellect to slice and dice
people. All of us get angry at times. But his anger was
different; it was volatile and dangerous. It was always there,
lurking right beneath the surface. It was part of him; it was
part of his shadow, and when he cast this shadow it created
dark and fearful places in which others had to work.

How did it matter? Individuals in his organization got to
the point where they did not want to risk sharing bad news
with him. Most chose not to disagree with a decision he made,
even when they thought it was going to take the company in
the wrong direction. Over time, men and women of the
company learned ways to get their work done around him, not
with him.

- Roberta was an executive with a large service-oriented
  company headquartered in the Midwest. From all outward
  appearances she seemed self-confident and self-assured—this
  was her persona. She made tough decisions in timely and
  effective ways. She served on the senior management team
  and was known as someone who would tell the emperor that
  he had no clothes. But she had another side, a side that I first
  came to know when I interviewed those who reported to her
  directly in preparation for a team development experience.
  Time after time, in one way or another, they would tell me
  about her insecurities that surfaced as anger, and they
  provided subtle but real behavioral examples to support their
  point of view. Their stories were compelling. As I worked with
  her over time I came to believe that these insecurities were
  part of her shadow—they were as much a part of her nature as
  were her great gifts. Because she did not acknowledge them,
  they grew "denser and blacker," and her insecurities were
  projected onto individuals and the organization she led. How
  so? Her employees described her as insecure, but, in truth, I
  do not remember working in any other organization in which
  individuals felt so anxious and insecure. They were carrying
  the executive's shadow; it was in them that her shadow
  became manifest.

- William was a clergy leader driven by an unexamined need to please those with whom he worked, and especially influential laypeople in his church. He was one of the warmest, most congenial people; he was supportive and encouraging. He listened well and was open to ideas, including ideas different from his own. He worked collaboratively—a vision for his church was co-created, and decisions on how to implement the vision were made collaboratively. So far, so good. The problem? He had such a huge fear of conflict or confrontation that if a powerful layperson expresses concern about the direction of the church, he quickly agreed to change it, and did so without any consultation with his staff. They constantly felt like the "rug was being pulled out from underneath them." His persona—the self he presented to the public—was strength grounded in compassion. Lurking in his shadow was a deep insecurity about his identity and, with it, a strong need to please the authority figures with whom he worked. He was not aware of his shadow. His tendency, instead, was to explain his change of direction as doing what was possible given the political realities. Did it matter? Of course it did. Members of William's staff suffered whiplash from the sharp turns taken. Finally, team members quit making any real commitment to a particular strategic direction.

None of these executives had gone down and in to get to know, much less befriend, their shadow. To the extent they knew they had a stranger dwelling within, they tended to deny it existed or work hard to keep it in the dark. But let me be clear: ignoring or denying our shadow is not an option. When we try, our shadow:

Pops out in ways that hurts us, others, and our organizations. This is what happened to the anger-based executive who used his anger to "slice and dice" people. When he was not expecting it, his right-beneath-the-surface anger would make an above-ground appearance. His expression of anger was toxic, not benign: the display of his anger could bring a good conversation about important organizational issues to a dead stop, and there were men and women in the organization who were not willing to speak the truth to him about concerns that were strategically important.

It gets projected onto others. This is the story of the second executive. Her employees described her as insecure, even paranoid. Though she did not mean to, and was probably not even aware of doing so, she projected her insecurities onto her team and they carried them for her—they were as insecure as they described her as being.

Our shadow grows denser and blacker when it is ignored. This is the story of the pastor. His need for approval slowly and over time tightened its grip on him. Our shadow gets less dense and lighter only when we acknowledge it and integrate it.

Some theorists argue that our shadow exists primarily in our unconscious. But my experience is that most of us are at least dimly aware of the "monsters" that dwell within, and that we can—with time and attention—learn to more clearly identify and name what lurks there. The things that "push our buttons" offer clues about what resides in our shadow. The things we don't like about others offer insights about our "monsters." The things we don't like about ourselves and try to keep hidden are clues that help us name our shadow. Our dreams can be a rich source of information.

Even when we are aware of these strangers that dwell within, integrating them is a slow, one-step at a time process. First we must acknowledge that we have a shadow. Then we must name it, call it what it is—deep-seated anger, insecurity, the need for affection and approval, or whatever. Along the way we must decide that we will not attempt to show our shadow the door. Rather, we must befriend it, just as we might welcome a stranger in our home—warily at first but warming up over time. As part of this decision we come to realize that our shadow has served us well, and that, in Jung's words, it "contains some childlike qualities which would in a way vitalize and embellish human existence" (Jacobi 1973, p. 113). Finally, we integrate our shadow and acknowledge, to ourselves and others, that we cast both light and shadow.

Going down and in to integrate our shadow is the hardest, most arduous part of the journey toward wholeness. On this leg of the journey we encounter some of the most difficult realities of our lives. It is a leg of the journey we do not want to take and we avoid it as long as we can. We keep hoping we can find an alternate route to living and leading as whole and authentic people. We finally commit to the journey when we realize we cannot be whole and free—cannot become the person we started out to be—unless we do.

Fusing Gifts and Limits

We must also integrate our gifts and limits on our journey. But just as I wish that I could only cast light, never shadow, so I also wish that I could discern and use my gifts in leadership activities and ignore or deny my limits. Slowly I have learned this is just not possible. You and I have a nature, a human nature, and one part of our DNA—one truth built into our core self—is that we have gifts *and* limits.

Warren Bennis told us "the point is not to become a leader. The point is to become yourself and to use yourself completely—all your gifts, skills and energies—to make your vision manifest" (1989, pp. 111–112). I am not sure what Bennis meant when he used the words gifts and skills, but for me the distinction between them is important. Gifts are those abilities or talents that have been part of us from the moment of our birth. They are the capacities we have that come naturally to us and abilities that have always been part of us.

The single best definition of gifts I have found is one offered by career counselor John Crystal: "gifts are those things you have always been able to do and don't remember learning how" (Wilson, 1987, pp. 132–133). This definition points to two critical dimensions of gifts: our gifts are things we have always been able to do—they are part of our nature, of our make up. They are natural abilities. They are not something we work hard to develop; they are not something we have to learn to do. One example from my life: I have always been able to organize work and events; I don't remember learning how. Gifts like this need to be honed and polished, but they do not have to be developed.

In contrast, skills are capacities we develop over time and often with considerable effort. There is clear and convincing evidence that we can and must develop new leadership skills over the course of our careers. Think of the leadership skills needed to help an organization chart a new direction, or the relationship skills needed to develop alignment with a new vision, or the competencies needed to help an organization navigate the whitewaters of change.

Morgan McCall describes the difference in gifts and skills this way, "The word development has two meanings. From one perspective, development involves identifying and then realizing potentialities—strengthening and polishing what already exists. From another perspective, development is about the acquisition of abilities—bringing new things into being." (1998, p. 11). To be effective in our leadership roles you and I need to both polish our gifts that are "in here" and develop new skills and competencies that are "out there."

One problem we face is when we have not acted as if both gifts and skills are important. The focus in much of the literature on leadership, and in most leadership development courses, has been on teaching individuals to go against their grain—go against their natural gifts—to develop abilities they do not have. It has been on developing new competencies and skills rather than on honing gifts. It has been on developing skills and perspectives to shore up weaknesses rather than acknowledging and learning to work with the interesting combination of gifts and limits, strengths and weaknesses that define us.

Even when we claim our gifts it is easy to ignore them or downplay their importance. It is easier for us to recognize and appreciate the skills and abilities we have worked hard to develop. Developing a new competency requires that we learn to do something that is not natural to us. Because we work hard, and spend so much time and energy developing these new skills and perspectives, we prize them more than the gifts that are part of us. We think anything earned by the sweat of our brow, developed though persistence and plugging along and lots of practice, must be more important than anything that comes easy to us. I know of one company president who discounts his gifts in imagining future scenarios for his company because they come so easily to him, and an executive who works for this president who downplays his natural ability to put "arms and legs" to the president's vision because "anyone can do that."

The tendency on our part to disown or deny our gifts is often reinforced in the organizations for which we work. One of the trends in corporations in recent years has been to define the competencies that individuals need to develop if they are to be effective in leadership roles and activities. The assumption underlying most competency models is that the skills identified as important can and must be learned, and good competency models identify the experiences in life and work from which the competency or skill can be learned. As we develop the competencies we need to correct a deficit we have, we get reinforced through positive feedback. If we are not careful, we begin to believe that the competencies we develop are more important to ourselves and to our organizations than the gifts with which we were born.

But discerning, claiming, and using our gifts is important in life and leadership:

- gifts help define true self; they help identify what is real and distinctive at the core of our being.
- different than skills, gifts can be more easily honed and polished and we can more easily develop a mastery of them.
- knowledge of our gifts will help identify what is right work. One definition of right work is work that allows us to use our gifts in ways that matter.
- our gifts define for each of us the distinct—perhaps unique—contribution we can offer to a practice of shared leadership or partnership. Partnerships work precisely because of the diversity of gifts individuals have that they offer to the accomplishment of leadership tasks.

There are two ways we can discern and claim our gifts. First, we can ask and answer the question of what has always come naturally for us. From life and work experiences—and reflection on them—I have identified some of those things I have "always been able to do and don't remember learning how." Though I am not an original thinker, I am gifted at synthesizing the ideas of others with my own thoughts, and doing so in a way that novel ideas can emerge. I am gifted at shepherding long-term projects—I can plan the work and work the plan. I am gifted at facilitating adult learning; I have honed this ability through the years, but I do not remember learning how to do it.

At other times I have recognized something as a gift only when someone else named it for me. I was in my early fifties when I first wrote a chapter for an edited book. The publisher selected a development editor to work with those of us who were writing chapters, a woman who was gifted in her ability to write and in her ability to coach aspiring authors. I remember the anxiety I felt when she first came to visit and review our initial drafts. Imagine, then, my surprise when she walked in my office and said, quickly and clearly, "There is not a lot I can add to your chapter. You have obviously had a lot of writing experience."

When I told her that this was the first chapter I had written for publication, she expressed surprise and then said, "You are a gifted writer. You need to write more."

Together my wife and I have six daughters, all now young adults. When they were younger I sometimes marveled at how different they were and I realized one way to understand those differences was to see that they had different gifts. At least two came into this world as organized human beings; to this day they easily and effectively organize all aspects of their life and work. One had more natural ability as an athlete. Several others are gifted at creative expression, though their art takes different forms. Several are gifted in their ability to relate to others in caring and compassionate ways. None of them took classes to learn to be organized or athletic or creative or compassionate; these are their innate gifts; it is part of their nature. To be sure, each worked hard to polish her gifts, but they did not start out their lives as empty vessels to be filled.

The good news is that we can ignore or deny our gifts, or misuse them, but we never rid ourselves of them. Gifts may lie dormant, but they don't die. One hope for each of us is that we will, as part of our journey to becoming ourselves, claim our giftedness.

We have gifts and we also have limits. By limits I do not mean those external constraints placed on individuals by something or someone outside of them. The "glass ceiling" has been an unjust corporate constraint on women for years. Racism and ageism have placed unfair constraints on people of color and older workers. The seemingly harmless dichotomy made in organizations between line and staff put artificial barriers on the contributions staff are allowed to make, on the gifts they are permitted to use. The labels we use and the realities to which the language points—like boss/subordinate or management/labor– limit the contribution of the many and favor the contribution of the few. Anything that "keeps others in their place" is this kind of constraint. These are not limits that are native to us, and not what I mean by limits.

Instead, by limits I mean those things that are as much a part of our identity, our human nature, as are our gifts. Just as we do not always discern and embrace our gifts, we do not always acknowledge and own our limits.

How do we discern our limits? In chapter three I described how hardships and the loss that accompanies them is a catalyst for learning about self and turning us toward home. The hardships we experience are often the times we run head-on into our limits. Through difficult, painful experiences we learn that we are finite, that we cannot be all and do all, that our gifts and skills are not always sufficient, that there are some good and important things that need to be done that we cannot and ought not do.

Another theme from CCL research is that we learn about our gifts and limits from a variety of other experiences—challenging assignments, bad bosses and difficult employees, and experiences outside of work that we find challenging and from which we learn and grow. Adversity comes in many forms, and from each we are offered the opportunity to identify and claim our limits.

There are ways to identify our limits besides bumping into them in difficult situations. We can identify limits from feedback from others, formal or informal. We identify our limits by reflecting on our experiences and realizing that no matter how hard we have tried there are some things we still cannot do. We discern our limits when we claim our gifts and realize that many of our gifts have a flip-side—one of the best preachers I have ever known knew that he was not a good listener. He told me that the reason he did not do one-to-one counseling is that he loved to talk too much.

Too many in leadership positions—in businesses, in nonprofit organizations, in governments, in churches and synagogues—either have not learned about their limits or they find it hard to acknowledge them. We assume that to be effective in leadership activities we must be all and do all. To admit there are things we ought not to do, we are not gifted at doing, seems an admission of failure. One example: during the time I lived in the southwest I came to know a company that was named after the man who founded it, and who was, for many years, the company president. He was, by most accounts, a creative genius. He was at his best—and his happiest—when he was in the lab developing new ideas and turning them into state-of-the-art products. It was in the lab that his great gifts were apparent to all who worked with him. As gifted as he was in the lab, he was equally limited in his ability to lead the company day-to-day. Asking him to work on leadership tasks or do the essential work of management was asking him to "go against his grain" and do work that did come easily or naturally to him. Ideally, this talented man would have continued to see himself as the chief innovation officer of the company, but because he founded it and wanted to run it, he tried to do so. He could not, or would not, acknowledge his limits. For a while it worked for him to run the organization, but not for the long haul. In the end, the company was purchased by a much larger company who had individuals gifted in leadership and management, and, as you might expect, the founder was given an opportunity to retire early.

Another example: a senior pastor of a large suburban church is a gifted preacher and teacher, but limited in his ability to do administrative work. There is an associate at the church who is the mirror opposite: gifted in administration but not so good at preaching. It could be an ideal for them to divide the work between them, but the senior pastor believes he should be able to do it all, and he thinks this is what his lay leaders expect of him. This belief is making him miserable; it is also making the associate and lay leaders in the church miserable.

Executives and managers who own their limits find the experience freeing. Several years ago I had the privilege of working one-to-one with the senior executive of a large corporation. As is the case with most of the coaching work I do, one of the first steps was to collect data about this executive from feedback instruments and from interviews with those who knew him well. The data I gathered was clear: this executive was gifted in imagining the future. He could articulate a clear and compelling vision of how his organization would look three to five years down the road. The ability to do this came easily to this executive; he described it as "coming naturally." No hard work, no sweat of the brow, about this. His limits were also clear from the feedback: he was not at all detail-oriented. This feedback only confirmed what he already knew. I asked him what he wanted to do to shore up this weakness, and his answer both surprised and enlightened me: "Nothing," he said, "absolutely nothing." He went on to tell me that early in his career he had spent an enormous amount of time and energy trying to become more detail-oriented, but to no avail. He finally decided that it was smarter to surround him with women and men who could put "arms and legs to my ideas."

Why was I surprised by his response? Because for years I had assumed that the purpose of leadership development was to identify and "fix" weaknesses. But this executive had learned to acknowledge he had limits, and there were things he ought not to do. He quit trying to fix himself; instead he owned his gifts and used them, and he acknowledged his limits and shared leadership with those who had gifts different from his own. Understanding that his gifts and his limits were both part of his nature freed this executive to be himself.

Other experiences have confirmed what I first realized so concretely from this executive. One mid-level manager with whom I worked while in Alaska was as good as anyone at analyzing and solving technical problems. Others in the organization used superlatives to describe him: "best engineer in the company," "best analytical mind that I have seen," "technically brilliant." He deserved this praise. He also deserved the other feedback he received: as good as he was as an engineer he was equally limited in his ability to deal with people. Could he develop his skill in building and maintaining relationships? Sure. But it would have been going against the grain for him. He was happier and more fulfilled working on engineering problems; it was the company, not him, who labeled him as "high potential" and who wanted him to climb the managerial ladder. He told me he felt a tremendous burden had been lifted off his shoulders when he decided to be a "high professional" rather than try to be "high potential."

Similarly, a highly accomplished woman I know is a gifted researcher and writer. She expresses herself beautifully in her writing; she knows this and claims it as gift. She also acknowledges her limits in expressing herself verbally, especially in front of groups of people. She once told me that she literally got sick the nights before a public presentation—it may just be that our bodies help us understand our limits. One form of expression is a gift for her; the other is a limit.

What all of this means, of course, is that our task is not to become an ideal person. Our task is to become our self—to become and be real, authentic, and whole. And whole does not mean perfect. It means being our true self and acknowledging that true self is a distinctive combination of gifts and limits.

Integrating All Our Energies

There is an Indian proverb that says we are all houses with four rooms—the physical, the mental, the emotional, and the spiritual—and that we need to spend time in each of these rooms every day. These rooms are all part of one house; these energies are all part of one person. True self is an integrated self; it is a whole self.

Often we act as if this were not true. As I suggested earlier, we think we can fragment or compartmentalize ourselves; we go to a doctor for physical problems, a therapist for emotional difficulties, school for mental or cognitive growth, a church or mosque or synagogue for spiritual development. We do not act as if these energies can or ought to be fused; we are not sure that wholeness is possible, or even if it is desirable.

This belief on our part is reinforced in the organizations for which we work. In the early part of the last century Frederick Taylor, the father of scientific management, said that factories needed workers who would use their brawn, not their brains—and Taylor thought he could calculate how much physical energy companies should expect from each worker each day. Taylor also argued that a thinking worker would be a dangerous worker. There was no perceived need in those days for a whole person to show up at work; indeed, workers were expected to compartmentalize themselves: take their physical selves to work but leave their head and heart and soul at home.

As we moved from the industrial era to the information age the needs of organizations changed. Companies needed individuals to bring their mental capacity to work—it was seen as a primary source of competitive advantage. The knowledge worker became an important asset, in some organizations the most important one. In these companies the use of mental energy was far more important than the use of physical energy.

Today, the needs of organizations and the expectations of workers have changed yet again. Organizations are realizing that to thrive today they need employees who offer the best they have within them. Our best self is our whole self. When we show up at work with our whole self we offer our heads and hearts and bodies and souls to the accomplishment of leadership tasks and the company's mission. A whole self who shows up at work will develop and share new knowledge, will work with deep commitment and motivation (remember, "emotion" and "motivation" come from the same root word), will find work meaningful and purposeful (finding meaning and purpose is a spiritual act), and will use physical energy.

Individual leaders may be technically brilliant (mental energy) and know all they need to know about their business, but if they lack emo-

106

tional intelligence (EQ), if they do not know themselves or how they impact others, they become candidates for derailment. A growing body of evidence suggests that leaders who are effective combine strong IQs with strong EQs—they fuse head and heart. Likewise, men and women may make enormous sacrifices for their work, literally exhaust themselves physically, but if the work does not have meaning or purpose, they die, metaphorically if not literally. Being engaged in leadership is stressful and requires emotional energy; when we are physically fit we are better able to handle these stresses. And so the story goes. We cannot be whole until we acknowledge the interrelatedness of all these energies and carefully and intentionally work to integrate them. Organizations simply do not get the best we have to offer when we show up as something less than a whole person.

Organizations need us to show up as whole men and women; it is also what we want for ourselves. We want work to matter and have purpose, not just provide a paycheck. We want an experience of community, not just a hierarchy where people are one-up or one-down. We want to make a life as much as we want to make a living. We want to show up and engage all of our energies, not just our mental or physical energy.

Charles Handy, noted author and successful business executive, said it this way: "we are not destined to be empty raincoats, nameless numbers on a payroll, role occupants, the raw material of economics or sociology, statistics in a government report ... there must be more to life than being a cog in someone else's great machine, hurtling God knows where" (1994, p. x). I think Handy has it right: we don't want to be a social security number or a brain without a name. We don't want to do work that is not meaningful, to be bored to death, to show up as half a person, be a cog in someone else's machine. Life is too short, and work occupies too much of our lives, for us to settle for that.

Being our true self in leadership roles requires that we become and be whole persons. Being whole requires fusing all of our energies.

From Wish to Action

There are some skeptics who will argue this focus on self is wrong-headed. They believe that focusing on oneself is selfish or, even worse, will lead to narcissism. My experience is just the opposite. In the years that I have worked with and gotten to know many leaders, I have met few, if any, for whom the primary issue was that they spent too much time in contemplation or on becoming themselves. I have found that self-doubt, and sometimes even self-loathing, is more of an issue than an inflated sense of self-love.

Regardless, we don't do deep inner work for ourselves alone. We don't reflect on the relationship of inner life and outer work, or do the hard work of journeying in and down to befriend our shadow, to inflate our ego or further develop the "cult of me." We work at integrating these different aspects of ourselves so that we will be able to engage in leadership as our whole and true self. We take this arduous and difficult journey so that we can be the person and leader that others want and expect us to be.

Being a Whole Person: A Reprise

One more time, what does it mean to be a whole person in leadership roles and activities?

It means knowing our inner life affects our outer work and is, in turn, affected by that work. And it means constantly paying attention to the interplay between these two.

It means recognizing and owning that we cast light and shadow, and it means befriending and integrating our shadow.

It means embracing our gifts and limits, our strengths and liabilities.

It means offering our whole self and all of our energies—our mind, our bodies, our spirit, and our heart—to the practice of leadership.

It means becoming the person we started out to be.

6. Staying True to Yourself

From time to time we have an experience where we say, "In that strategic planning meeting I was myself. I stayed true. I did not hide. I stated my position and shared my values clearly and cleanly. My leadership was rooted in my identity." We found our true north. Role and soul were connected. We found home and want to stay there. We wonder if it is possible.

To borrow the language of Wendell Berry's Jayber Crow, we ask if we can stay on the "King's Highway" and avoid any future "dangers, toils and snares"? We wonder if we can now find a way around the "Dark Woods of Errors." We ask if we can now engage in leadership as whole and authentic people and not have to experience Hell or Purgatory— being dissolved and shaken—again.

In a word, the answer is no.

At least the answer has been "no" in my life. The decision to engage in leadership wholly and authentically is one I must make over and over and over again. The decision of whether to show up as true self or false self is a decision I make several times a day. The decision of whether or not to collude, to say yes when I want to say no, is a decision I make in almost every meeting of consequence I attend. The process of discerning my gifts, understanding when and how I project my shadow, knowing how to work with my limits, and deciding to use all my "gifts and skills and energies" in service of an organization is an on-going, lifelong process.

You and I experience the deep connection between role and soul, and then lose it as we give in to one fine seduction or another—a new position is offered us that strokes our ego even though deep down we know the work is not right for us, a new leadership opportunity is offered us in a civic club or in our community that is ego-satisfying but asks that we play a role rather than be ourselves, or once again we catch ourselves being the leader others expect us to be rather than being the person we are. It is not easy, this quest to become and stay authentic.

But since we have found a way to true self and spent time there, we at least know it exists, are able to recognize it when we see it, and somewhat better able to find our way back to it. The trips we have made home to the center of our being provide us some sense of when our compass is pointing in the right direction, but even this does not always keep us from going in circles or doubling back.

There are certain practices that can be used to help keep who we are connected to what we do. Think of these practices as an internal GPS system that points us to true north, and this GPS comes with a small quiet voice that lets us know when a wrong turn has been taken or when a new calibration is needed. But don't think of the practices as providing an easy or safe path. These are not helpful hints for hurtful habits. There will still be "dangers, toils and snares." The path will go again through the "Dark Woods of Errors." You and I will again experience purgatory and hell, but not necessarily in that order. But the practices will keep us at home more of the time, and help us find our way back when we stray.

The Work Before the Work

Maybe the single most important thing I have learned about staying true is to do the work before the work. I learned the importance of this from a poem by a 4th century Taoist, Chuang Tzu, called "The Woodcarver"—Parker Palmer introduced me to this poem and to the idea of doing the work before the work. Palmer has written about the poem is several of his books; here is my short version of the story: Khing, a master carver, was commanded to make a bell stand of precious wood. Before starting this work Khing knew he had important inner work to do. In his own words, he did three things: he guarded his spirit and did not spend it on trifles, he fasted in order to put his heart at rest, and he forgot all thoughts of praise and criticism. When Khing did these things "all that might distract me from the work had vanished" and "I was collected in the single thought of the bell stand." After guarding and fasting and forgetting, Khing went to the forest, had a live encounter with a tree, and from this encounter came the bell stand that left all those who saw it so "astonished" that they said "it must be the work of spirits."

Astonishing work does not happen as a matter of course; it does not come with the ebb and flow of life—not for Khing, not for me, not for you. Instead, astonishing work, including being effective in the work of leadership, happens when we take time to do the inner work before we engage the outer work. Perhaps you would use different verbs than Khing to describe the inner work you must do, but his verbs work for me. I have them posted on my computer so that I am reminded of them often. Before beginning any particular workshop or retreat or consulting assignment I spend some time alone and ask myself:

- What do I need to do to guard my spirit, my energy, that breath of life inside me? How can I make sure I will not spend it on trifles, on things that are not to the point?
- From what do I need to fast in order to put my heart at rest? What do I need to make sure I do not over-consume so that I will not be anxious and restless?
- What do I need to forget if I am to have a live encounter with those others with whom I am engaged in a leader development course or leader formation retreat? Do I, like the woodcarver, need to forget thoughts of praise or criticism? Do I need to lay aside any concern about end-of-course evaluations or future funding for the program?

Khing had seven days to do this inner work before he entered the forest. I cannot imagine having the luxury of that much time, but then again, I suspect having seven days is not a requirement. What is important is the recognition that staying true to our self takes more time than the three minutes I sometimes give it while moving hurriedly from one meeting or experience to another. What is important is that I adopt a disciplined and regular practice of doing the inner work before I engage my outer work.

111

The Work Between the Work

A more recent realization for me is that I need to build into my schedule times in which I quit working so that my soul—my true self—has time to catch up with the rest of me.

I realized I needed this—not for the first time, but again—while reading and pondering the story of a South American tribe who, in the middle of a journey, would stop to allow time for their souls to catch up. They would do this regardless of the importance of the task, the distance they still had to travel, or the expectation of important others who thought they should continue to walk.

In my life and work I haven't done this often; I don't think many in our culture do. Instead, as author Wayne Muller points out:

> Our culture invariably supposes that action and accomplishment are better than rest, that doing something—anything—is better than doing nothing. Because of our desire to succeed, to meet the ever-growing expectations, we do not rest. Because we do not rest, we lose our way ... instead, as it all piles endlessly upon itself, the whole experience of being alive begins to melt into one enormous obligation. It becomes the standard greeting everywhere: "I am so busy" ... We say this with no small degree of pride, as if our exhaustion were a trophy, our ability to withstand stress a mark of real character. The busier we are, the more important we seem to ourselves, and, we imagine, to others [*Sabbath*, pp. 1, 2].

When I read these passages I knew instantly it was relevant to me and the life I was living. I grew up with a mother who loved to say that we could not go swimming or out to play or on vacation until "all the cows are in the barn." The way I translated this then, and understand it now, is that I could not stop to rest or relax, much less play, until everything was marked off my "to do" list. The problem, of course, is that this never happens; the cows are never all in the barn. There is always something left to do. I am so busy. And my father was fond of saying "idle hands are a devil's workshop." I do not remember him having idle time. If he was not at work, he was working around the house. I remember him kidding, but only partially, that Labor Day meant time to labor around the house. He was so busy.

The organizations in which I have worked—as an employee and as a consultant—often reinforce this cultural norm and my own personal tendency. Multi-tasking is encouraged. Efficiency is prized. Doing more with less is expected. Speed, doing work quickly, is the coin of the realm. Working long hours is the standard. I remember in my first corporate job the first piece of advice I received was "don't go home before your boss." In my second job my boss told me that no one would ever tell me I was doing too much—traveling too much, training too much, working too many hours. He told me I was responsible for managing myself—including my time and the hours I worked. But it was like telling a drunk that he should take care of himself while he was living in a bar.

Why? Because the organizational expectations fit with the internal pressure I felt and carried with me. Not only did I believe I must mark everything off my "to do" list before I left work, but I also I lived and worked the injunction to "hurry up." Hurry up to get one task done so I could move to another. Hurry up to finish one conversation so I could start another. Get this meeting over; I have another I must attend. No time to really engage the moment, much less enjoy it; there are other tasks to accomplish, clients to call or see, miles to go before I sleep. The organization encouraged me to keep my "RPMs" spinning at a fast pace; it was how I had gotten used to living and working.

All of my experience says I am not alone in this. Leaders from every sector with whom I work give the "I am so busy" response when asked how they are doing—it is the answer they want to give and are expected to give. They seem to live with the motto "I am what I do" (or as someone said, "we are human doers more than human beings"), and thus it follows that the more I do the more I am. For years we have had a name for the phenomena of always being "on" with a Blackberry: "crackberry" users. We are always on call, available 24/7. I recently worked with an executive of a major U.S. firm who sheepishly acknowledged that he brought along and checked his Blackberry on his Friday night dates with his wife. Who among us doesn't know the story of a smart phone user who does not finish a Thanksgiving meal without checking their phone, or the parent who spends way too much time on a family vacation checking and responding to messages rather than being fully present with family? More recently the phenomenon has been texting. A recent article in a local newspaper told the story of a young person who had sent over 6,000 text messages in a single month. She acknowledged that she was addicted and she had a dawning awareness that the sheer volume of her texting "might be a problem."

The result of our tendency toward busyness is that we never get caught up with the information and tasks with which we are inundated minute-by-minute, much less have time for deep nourishing rest. We kid that the "hurrieder we go the behinder we get," but it is no joke. Trying to meet ever-growing expectations, we travel on with our intellect, our ego, our strong will, but not with our soul or true self—it gets left behind. When our soul—our life-giving core—gets left behind, we lose our way. Soul and role are disconnected. Who we are is not connected to what we do.

We need to do what the South American tribe knew they must do— stop to allow our souls to catch up. Wayne Muller says it this way, "If busyness has become a kind of violence, we do not have to stretch our perception very far to see that Sabbath time—effortless, nourishing rest—can invite a healing of this violence ... Sabbath is a way of being in time *where we remember who we are* ... like a path in the forest, Sabbath creates a marker for us so, if we are lost, *we can find a way back to our center*" (1999, pp. 5, 6, italics mine).

In some religious traditions Sabbath is thought of as a day. For the purposes of this book and your life, think of it is a metaphor, not as a day but as an experience of deep nourishing rest. For some of us this means a few minutes of breathing space during the day, for others it is a full-day of rest each week, and still for others deep nourishing rest requires a longer sabbatical. However long, Sabbath time allows our soul a chance to catch up so that we can remember who we are and engage in leadership as ourselves—our authentic and whole selves.

And if we do not take time for deep and nourishing rest? One of the lessons nature offers us is that for many plants a time of dormancy in winter is necessary if they are to bear fruit in spring. And so it is with us: we must have time to lie fallow, time for our true self to catch up with the rest of us, if we are to become and be the person we started out to be, and to be whole and authentic leaders.

The Work During the Work, Part I: Becoming Unintentional Contemplatives

Life and leadership provide us experiences to contemplate, whether we want to or not. A good friend undercuts us, a strategy we had carefully considered leads down the wrong path, a relationship we value blows up in our face, we get turned down for an assignment we really wanted, we wake up in a meeting and realize we are saying yes when we want to say no. Life throws us curve balls; ready or not here they come.

If we are awake—not in denial or blind to the lessons that might be learned—experiences like these force us to contemplate. We ask questions of meaning. We ponder what happened. We dig beneath the surface. We question our assumptions, our motives, and our values. We wonder where to find our self in the midst of anger or embarrassment. Hopefully, our contemplation will help us discern new realities about who we are at our core.

Several years ago I failed to get a coaching assignment to work with a senior executive in a major corporation. I expected to get it. I wanted to do the work and it was at a time when I needed the income the work would have produced. When the human resource director called to tell me another coach had been selected, I asked her if she had any feedback that would be helpful to me. Though I do not remember her exact words, she said something like, "the executive is a hard-nosed, arrogant, 'take no prisoners' kind of guy, and I think you have too much of a gentle spirit to work with him." This is not what I expected or wanted to hear. My initial response was to deny what she said was true. This brief conversation turned me into an unintentional contemplative. The more I considered her comment and reflected on what I knew to be true about who I am at the core of my being, the more I realized she was right. I am not as effective coaching the kind of executive she described. The illusion that I can effectively coach any executive at any time is an illusion that did not serve me well. Now I feel freer to work with those executives who are a better match with who I am, and freer to decline work when I know it is not right for me.

I have a friend who was struggling to make meaning of a curve ball recently thrown her way. She is a gifted consultant and trainer, one who has a history of doing top-notch work with clients, and who has the background and experience for a contract she did not get. She did not understand. She felt victimized. She was discouraged and angry. The situation turned her into a contemplative. It is still too early in the experience and her emotions are too raw, for me (or she) to know what lessons will be learned or whether she will pierce any illusions she carries about herself.

Learning the right lessons from difficult experiences is not automatic. We can respond by becoming cynical or discouraged. We can experience an embarrassing event and never touch the reality of who we are. Or we can ask the right questions, be open to learning about ourselves, and get beyond the unhelpful illusions we carry about ourselves, the other person, and the situation. Reality is always better than illusion—often harder to embrace, but always better.

In the third chapter I shared stories about a company president, Jim, and the leadership lessons he learned from the personal trauma of a heart attack, and the story of Steve Job's commencement address when he shared his story of "love and loss," the story of Jobs starting, building and then getting fired from Apple Computer. These experiences turned these two men into unintentional contemplatives. They each learned and grew from the experience because they turned and faced into them, asked questions of meaning and purpose, and allowed the experiences to strip them of illusions they carried about themselves.

When finishing his story Steve Jobs said, "Sometimes life hits you in the head with a brick. Don't lose faith." To this I add, and don't lose this opportunity to learn and grow from it. In taking this awful tasting medicine we can learn crucial lessons about our whole and authentic self.

The Work During the Work, Part II: Becoming Intentional Contemplatives

There is also contemplative work that individuals do intentionally as they engage in leadership. Simply stated, it is reflecting and becoming self-aware, including being aware of when role and soul are connected and when they are not.

Not all executives have or develop the capacity to be reflective. William was the new president of a moderately large and rather complex organization. Before being chosen to lead this company he had been a very successful leader in another organization where he had a noted and honored track record. He was one of the most principled, value-centered executives I have known; early on he made a decision that would cost the new company significant income but would uphold their core values. He did not blink. During his tenure as president the new organization grew, expanded its services, developed its staff, and cemented its reputation as a leading provider of services in its field—all the external measures of success improved. William made notable contributions to these improvements. He was tremendously gifted, but like the rest of us, he had a blind spot. He would "flash" on people, cutting them off in midsentence to tell them that their idea would not work and that there was no need to discuss it further. It didn't happen often. It didn't need to. The story of his "flashing" quickly made the rounds of the organization and those we typically called "followers" decided that the safe and secure way to live was to keep some of their most important ideas to themselves.

William did not know the impact of his practice of leadership on others. William's illusion was that his behavior was both appropriate and benign—appropriate because he was saving the organization time and energy when he cut off a conversation that he knew was going nowhere, and benign because he saw no ill-effects of his behavior.

Though successful on many levels, William was unaware of how his behavior cut off innovation, stifled creativity, and undermined employee morale. He did not reflect on or examine his behavior, and as far as I could tell, he did not do contemplative work before or during the work. If he had, he would have found more effective ways of responding to creative ideas, the organization would have been more innovative, and employees would have been more inspired.

There are many executive leaders like William who are not that reflective or self-aware—you and I know them by name, and sometimes the name is our own. Like William, we have not learned to catch ourselves in the act. We have not developed the art or practice of being intentionally contemplative. We do not realize in the moment that soul and role are separated. And we may work in organizations where no premium is placed of developing this capacity.

This work during the work means reflecting on the fly and developing self-awareness as we go. It is learning while doing. It is self-monitoring and self-moderating. It is noticing in the moment that we are not staying true to ourselves and deciding to change, on the spot.

Part Two: The Journey to Authentic Leadership

Bill George, former president of Medtronics, and three colleagues wrote an article "Discovering Your Authentic Leadership," in which they described the importance of self-awareness. They wrote:

> When the 75 members of the Stanford Graduate School of Business Advisory School of business were asked to recommend the most important capability for leaders to develop, their answer was nearly unanimous: *self-awareness*. Yet many leaders, especially those early in their careers, are trying so hard to establish themselves that they leave little time for self-exploration. They strive to achieve success in tangible ways that are recognized by the external world—money, fame, power, status, or a rising stock price. Often their drive enables them to be professionally successful for a while, but they are unable to sustain that success. As they age, they may find that something is missing in their life and realize that they are holding back from being the person they want to be. *Knowing their authentic selves requires the courage and honesty to open up and examine their experiences.* As they do so, leaders become more humane and willing to be vulnerable [2007, pp. 3–4, italics mine].

Examining our experiences is another name for the contemplative work we need to do while working. It is work that requires courage and honesty. It requires us to develop our EQ, or emotional intelligence, our awareness of our own inner emotional terrain and how our inner life impacts our outer work, including how it impacts those we are leading. EQ also includes an awareness of and appreciation for the feelings and inner life of others.

We have also learned that men and women who are not self-observant and self-aware, who do not develop their EQ, are candidates for derailment. Derailment, a term coined by researchers at the Center for Creative Leadership, can mean a person gets fired, but more often it means that their career stalls, they get demoted, or they get moved sideways into unfulfilling work. I have even known executives for whom derailment meant getting "kicked upstairs" into a job where there was no real work to do.

How was the lack of self awareness demonstrated in these derailed men and women? Here are but a few of the things that were said about these once "high potential" individuals: "She was cool, aloof and arrogant"; "He used his intelligence to make others look stupid"; "She would turn on dime—one moment she would be warm and the next she would slice and dice people with her anger"; "He put down people—he called them out—in public"; "She just did not really trust others. She was one of those who thought that if a report was going to be done right she had to do it. And she didn't seem to understand what impact this had on her people." Even if these individuals knew something about the interplay of their inner life and their external work, their self-awareness was not what it needed to be. Unwittingly and unintentionally, they inflicted their unexamined experiences on others.

The Work During the Work, Part III: Asking Others to Help Us

Sometimes self-reflection is not enough. It is important, but not sufficient. We don't realize that in a particular experience we are not showing up as a real person, that others see us as inauthentic. We have blind spots, and we will retain them unless and until our traveling companions are willing to tell us the truth about who we are and about how our behavior impacts them.

In organizations this kind of truth-telling has a name: feedback. A story about the impact of feedback underlines its importance: Daniel was a bright, hard-charging, aggressive new boss, asked to turn around a unit of an organization whose business was in a tailspin. After a year the business had improved but Daniel was in trouble. I was asked to give him feedback from a multi-rater instrument so he could begin to see himself as others saw him. The feedback Daniel received highlighted his strengths: he was seen by others as strategic, resourceful, resilient, and willing to do whatever it took to get his agenda accomplished. His weaknesses were just as glaring: others told him he was not good at building and maintaining relationships, that he was abrasive, that all too often he put down his employees in public, and that he was overly-ambitious.

He was surprised by this feedback. He had expected his accomplishments and the improvements made to the bottom-line under his watch would lead to positive feedback, and only positive feedback. He spent the first part of our session either denying the feedback or explaining it away. I finally said something to Daniel like, "I hope you will pay attention; this is maybe a blind spot you have. This feedback says your colleagues feel demeaned and diminished by you. They don't feel like their contributions are acknowledged. They are saying that you think this turnaround is all about you." Daniel struggled with the message but finally said something like, "I sure haven't seen myself that way ... I must be in denial ... I had no idea how self-serving I looked to others." It was at this point Daniel became, if only for this experience, a contemplative. It was also at this moment I began to hope that change was possible.

I had a similar experience with a clergy leader with whom I worked as a coach. He went to a new appointment full of excitement, with successful ideas from his previous appointments that he was sure would work in the new, and with a determination to "jump start" his new church with a bold vision, a church he saw as a "sleeping giant"—full of potential but stuck in place. Unfortunately, his vision for the church, a vision he was able to beautifully articulate, was not shared by the lay leaders of the church. He encountered resistance to the direction he had in mind; he dealt with the resistance by becoming more forceful. This curve ball thrown his way did not cause him to become contemplative. He did not get beyond his illusion that he was right, skillful enough, and politically astute enough, to carry the day. He had a hard time acknowledging that his behavior—the way he was "casting his vision"— was a cause of the problem; instead, he labeled the lay leaders "elderberries" and decried the fact that they were resistant to change. Slowly, and after lots of feedback that was not fun to hear, this good man realized the how of casting a vision is as important as the vision itself.

I know a lot of people like Daniel and this clergy leader who have a hard time hearing this kind of feedback; I am one of them. And I know, from hard experience, that it takes practice to listen to rather than deny feedback like this. But I know that receiving honest feedback on an ongoing basis is one way to maintain self-awareness and to keep who we are connected to what we do.

One reason that Daniel and other leaders in positions of power do not receive the feedback they need and deserve is that those who are called subordinates hesitate to tell the truth to them about the impact of their behavior. It only takes one story making the rounds of a messenger getting shot to send others into hiding. These stories, like the story of William's flashes, make the rounds faster than the speed of light.

This problem is exacerbated for Daniel and others as they climb the organizational ladder—the higher individuals go in an organization the less honest feedback they receive. They become isolated from those doing the work on the ground; their offices are off limits—either literally in a fortress-like bunker on the top floor that can only be reached by a special elevator, or figuratively with less tangible but equally real barriers. Too often, self-awareness goes down as a person goes up the organizational ladder.

The way for the leader-who-is-an-executive to get the feedback she needs is to ask for it, to probe for it, to do it so often it becomes a normative part of her relationships, and then to receive it graciously. Not joyously, but graciously. Over time, people will expect to be asked, and know that when they provide helpful feedback they will be appreciated and not punished. And this information too will circulate around the office like wildfire.

Asking for feedback is its own art form; it is hard to master and hard to do. Without thought, the request for feedback can sound more manipulative than a request for honest assessment. "That meeting went well, didn't it?" is a very different kind of question than the request, "Give me feedback about how I managed the meeting." And "That confrontation with Roger did not go well, huh?" is a different kind of request than "Tell me what I can do to be more effective the next time I have a situation like the one I just had with Roger." Asking for feedback with specific, honest questions or requests generates the most helpful data.

Even as we need feedback about blind spots that hinder our effectiveness, we also need feedback about strengths we have. I remember the time a colleague asked if she could observe me facilitating a particular program because she had heard I did it well. After the session, she gave me feedback noting the particular things I had done which affirmed my gifts as a facilitator.

I was surprised because I had never considered facilitating one of my gifts. From my perspective, it was simply something I did as part of my work. For sure it was not a skill I had learned in one workshop or another. Because I did not see facilitating as a gift, I only used it as a small part of my work. I did not try to extend the times and ways I would take on this role. Hearing the feedback made me think more broadly about this skill and how I might incorporate it in more of my work. Not recognizing something as a gift can be its own blind spot and limit the

121

ways we choose to fully use it. Receiving feedback about our gifts also turns us into a contemplative.

A Reprise

There is no magic pill we can take that will allow us to stay true to ourselves, but there are practices that can help. To summarize:

We can do the work before the work. Each of us needs time to do our inner work—some version of guarding and fasting and forgetting—before we engage our outer work.

We need to do the work between the work. At times we need to slow down, stop work, rest, and give our souls time to catch up with the rest of us.

We need the experience of becoming unintentional contemplatives. When life throw us curve balls, we need to do more than just duck. We need to learn from them, ask questions of meaning, dig beneath the surface, and clarify what is really important to us.

We need to become intentional contemplatives. We need to develop our emotional intelligence, to become more self-aware and more aware of our impact on others. We need to get beyond illusions we carry about ourselves and embrace reality.

We need to ask others to help us. We need feedback to help us recognize our blind spots. We need trustworthy traveling companions who will hold us accountable for showing up as a whole and true self. And we need these companions to name gifts we have yet to recognize or embrace.

7. *Authentic Leadership and Power*

Milton was an important client with whom I worked. He was an executive vice president of an oil and gas company, and as such was the one responsible for a major part of the company's operations. He was an effective problem-solver, a forceful manager, and by almost all external measures, successful. He appeared confident and self-assured; he was willing to step up to the plate and make tough decisions. He was a take-charge kind of guy. And he had a need to let me know he was the boss. My first conversation with him went something like this:

> HIM: Sit down [this after I walked into his office for the first time. No word of welcome. No getting up to shake my hand]. I have a question for you: how much oil have you ever found in your life?
> ME [after an awkward pause]: Not any.
> HIM: That's right. The only oil you ever found was under your car, right?
> ME [after laughing nervously]: Yeah, I guess you are right.
> HIM: I asked you that as a way of letting you know that as long as you are here you work for me. You understand that?
> ME: I understand what you are saying.
> HIM: That's all. You can go now [and at that point he turned away and started dialing someone on his phone].

I was stunned. I did not know what to think. But as I worked with him—and with one of his direct employees who was actually my client—over a period of several years, and as I noticed how often he let me and others know in no uncertain terms that he was the boss, I began to think that if I could peel back layers I would find a threatened and insecure man. The insecurity was part of his substrate, part of his shadow, part of himself that he never got to know, at least as far as I know. His insecurity was not benign; it was toxic. It was, in my opinion, the reason he was so quick to pull out a stick (and he used it far more than he used a carrot), and he used it in a way that poisoned relationships.

A power dynamic exists in every relationship. There is no way around it. It existed in my relationship with Milton; it exists in my relationship with my wife. But it is a difficult dynamic to acknowledge, much less talk about. I have been on many different work teams in the course of my career, managed different groups of people, been a team development consultant to different senior management teams, served on various boards, and enjoyed many meaningful relationships, and not in a single one has the issue of power and its impact on the functioning of the team or group been surfaced, even though it is usually somewhat evident.

One of the reasons the reality of power is not acknowledged is that it is thought of in negative terms. People who thirst for power are frowned on. No one wants to be seen as power hungry. There are enough examples of people like Milton who misuse power to make even the most trusting person wary.

But there is an important difference in coercive power, power that is based on having a carrot or stick and personal power, power that accrues to individuals who author their own lives, who are perceived as authentic, and who are granted authority by others.

In this chapter the difference in coercive power and personal power is explored, and each is related to becoming one's true self and an authentic leader.

A Case Study: Coercive Power

When I entered the field of management and Organization Development (OD) one of my first corporate clients was a large and well-known aerospace company. The intervention, designed by the internal OD manager, was intended to change the prevailing practice of management in the organization. I was asked to help with the implementation.

The company's practice of leadership and management needed to change, I was told, because the business environment had changed.

This is not unusual; often it is an external factor that causes a company to begin a process of renewal. In this case and for the foreseeable future, this aerospace company was going to have to rely less on defense-related business and grow its commercial business. There was a shared agreement, at least among the top executives, that to succeed in this new environment the company was going to have to become more entrepreneurial, create more cooperation across functional groups that had operated like separate fiefdoms, and get better cooperation from all workers. Long before cross-functional, self-managed work teams were popular or prevalent, this company decided to move in that direction.

The intervention in this company started with an organizational survey and from it we learned that information flowed top-down, that decisions were pushed up, that relationships throughout the organization were characterized by fear and mistrust (the paper trail in this company was a long one; the tip most-often passed on to all those entering the management ranks was CYA—"Cover Your Ass."). We also learned the primary reason for the fear and mistrust was that too many bosses used coercive power.

Coercive power is defined as having "power over," and having enough of it so that the other—subordinate, peer, student, child—can be manipulated, cajoled, or forced into acting in a prescribed way. A prerequisite to coercive power is having something the other wants (a carrot) or something they fear (a stick). As long as you have something I desire or something I fear losing, you have coercive power over me. The rewards and punishments can range from the subtle to the severe— from dangling a plum assignment in front of me to promising me a promotion, from ignoring me to threatening to fire me.

In the aerospace company it was a stick, not a carrot, that was used to coerce, and the managers had a name for it: "my way or the highway." I was introduced to this phrase in this company, and I heard it a lot.

The threat of the highway worked because the highway was something employees feared. Economic times were tough and high-paying hourly jobs were hard to come by. Employees who were afraid they could not find another job were willing to be coerced. A stick is more likely to work when the economy is down.

Many managers in this company welcomed the new management

practices and worked hard to become the kind of trust-based, participatory manager the company needed. Others did not. They had grown comfortable with the old ways of managing, and they liked using coercive power. They honestly believed that "my way or the highway" was the only way to insure that employees would be productive and that quality would be maintained. The complaint I heard most often from these supervisors and managers was that if the company took away their stick—and with it their ability to coerce—it would take away their power.

This is a lament I have heard often through the years. I have heard it from parents, from teachers, from school administrators, from supervisors in a variety of organizations, from clergy leaders, from company executives. The underlying assumption is that for managers—or for any of us—the ability to reward or punish is our only source of power. Take away the carrot and stick and you render us powerless, or so we think.

What the old-school managers in the aerospace company failed to notice and take into account is the negative consequences of using of coercive power.

The first problem with the use of coercive power is it can only work when the other is dependent or afraid. When employees are dependent on their manager for approval or for a tacit possibility of advancement they will allow themselves to be coerced. And when they fear the stick the managers have—from being given a less-than-challenging assignment to being told to hit the highway—coercive power will work. Coercive power works only when the other is willing to swap his or her freedom for what appears to be safety and security.

"So what," one of the aerospace mangers asked, "what's wrong with employees being a little bit afraid? Fear can be a powerful motivator." Here's what's wrong with it: with dependency comes avoidance of even appropriate risk-taking, the desire to hide mistakes, behavior designed solely to gain approval, the decision to tell the boss only what she wants to hear, and the decision to keep true self hidden or at least out of sight. With fear comes CYA behaviors, an unwillingness to proactively try new things, and often a decision to do only what one is told, no more, no less. Coercive power encourages collusion.

Employees who are dependent or afraid usually show up at work "wearing someone else's face." They create and show up as a false self because of their hope for the reward or their fear of the punishment.

But it is not just the individual who is affected; having employees who are dependent or afraid does not build a culture or a company capable of creating or accomplishing a vision of greatness.

Coercive power also bends the manager—the one using coercive power—out of his or her original shape. Not always, but much of the time it is the weak-ego person, a person anxious about his or her identity, who tends to use coercive power, and the use of coercive power often masks underlying issues of insecurity. Coercive power, power that comes with the position but does not belong to the person, allows a manager to show up as someone he is not—a strong person who can make things happen. In contrast, a person who claims and uses her personal power is a person who authorizes herself and shows up as true self.

Another problem with coercive power is that any time coercive power flows one way in a relationship, resentment and hostility flow the other. Sometimes the resistance is subtle and hard to see, at other times it erupts in the form of open rebellion. One of the more subtle and pernicious forms of resistance used by individuals has a name—malicious obedience. Malicious obedience is doing what we are ordered to do even when it is wrong and we know it will not work.

Malicious obedience is hard to see; open resistance is not. Some of the managers and executives in the aerospace company understood the dynamic of open resistance and knew the resistance was a response to their use of coercive power. These were the managers open to change. Others saw the open resistance and concluded the only appropriate response was to ratchet up the coercion, to use a bigger stick. This led, of course, to more hostility and resentment. This is why the shop floor often looked and felt more like a battle zone than a productive and satisfying workplace. Creating less-hierarchical, more trust-based work teams was not possible in that kind of environment.

A final consequence of using coercive power is that even when it leads to compliance, it does not engender real commitment. Too many managers and executives think commitment can be bought. The question becomes: what size stick (or carrot) do I need to get them to commit? Author and consultant Peter Block says, "People in power [those who use coercive power] despair of finding commitment without resorting to devices designed to get someone to do something" (2002, p. 55). This, he adds, begins the "commercialization of commitment."

When old-school managers at the aerospace company talked among themselves about what size stick it would take for employees to give up any participation in the management process, to swap their freedom for a promise of security, they were not talking about commitment but about making a deal. Making a deal does not produce the kind of commitment that gives energy and vitality to work or relationships. It does not produce commitment from the inside-out. And it does not lead to the kind of commitment needed if managers, leaders, and workers are to work together to accomplish leadership tasks—co-create a vision or sense of direction, maintain alignment, clarify and act on core values, and produce lasting and useful change. Commitment comes from choice, not coercion; it can never be commercialized.

Ironically, sticks and carrots are not, in the final analysis, real sources of power. Managers can use coercive power only when followers let them. This means it is always followers who decide whether the manager has coercive power. Coercive power is on loan from followers, and followers can call the note on a moment's notice.

The managers and executives at the aerospace company acknowledged and talked about the way followers carried the note. Some told me they realized that when the economy was good and jobs were available at other aerospace companies in the area "my way or the highway" did not work. In good economic times, employees would call the note by leaving for another company. But employees sometimes called the note long before they walked out they door. They "fired" the coercive boss by granting him no authority. Or they tuned him out. Or they avoided him, psychologically if not physically.

When Using Coercive Power Is Not So Clear

In the aerospace company the use of coercive power was evident. It was evident in the rewards given and in the punishments meted out. Managers in this company, and especially those on the shop floor, made no attempt to conceal their stick. On the contrary, they wanted it seen and feared.

Usually the use of coercive power is much more obtuse. I learned this during one of my managerial assignments at the Center for Creative

Leadership. In my group I hoped to create a trust-based, collaborative leadership process. I wanted the direction to emerge from our interaction, wanted commitment, not compliance, to our strategies and goals, and knew I needed the best I could get from my colleagues if we were to succeed in a very fast-changing environment. I did not want to use coercive power; I wanted to be an important voice in the conversations and wanted my voice to have influence, but I did not want to use a stick or carrot to get my way. If I had power I wanted it because those who worked with me granted me authority because they perceived me to be authentic and trustworthy.

But I did have coercive power. Even if I never wanted to use it, I had it. It was a reality I did not easily or readily acknowledge. The fact that I was the one who could recommend annual salary increases, a colleague for a promotion, or provide interesting assignments, meant that I had carrots. The fact that I could fire an employee, or assign less interesting work, meant that I had sticks. Those with whom I worked knew this.

My hope was to minimize the impact of the sticks and carrots. I was careful not to use coercive power to get my way or force my will. I do not think those who worked with me were either afraid of me or dependent on me, though, like other groups with whom I have worked, we never discussed the dynamic of power. At the aerospace company coercive power was used in a way that it became corrosive; I always hoped that this was not true in the group I managed.

Collusion Revisited

One of the themes running through this book is that collusion often happens in relationships and in organizational life—whether the organization is a neighborhood, school, business, or not-for-profit organization.

The case study of the aerospace company helps connect the dots of power and collusion: the managers had coercive power only when employees allowed it. It is always much easier to allow it and harder to resist coercive power when it is part of the management culture, but still, without really meaning to, or being fully aware of doing so, employees at the aerospace company allowed, even unintentionally encouraged, their managers and leaders to engage in the coercive behaviors they said they did not like. They allowed it because they were dependent or afraid. They allowed it because their safety and security—or what they thought was security—were more important than their freedom. They allowed it because they did not have the courage to say "no" when they wanted to say "no."

I remember, all too well, times in my career when I have colluded. I remember a time at CCL, for example, when the way we were organized to accomplish our work was being reviewed and changes were in the offing. I was not involved in any of the conversations. When my boss called me in to tell me about the realignment I went in with an attitude. I was upset I had not been involved in the process and I was determined to tell him so. But he started the conversation with a statement of how much I was going to gain from the new structure—including a nice raise and a new title—and my determination to protest the process quickly faded. I allowed myself to be seduced by a very nice carrot. In one way, my story is very different than the story of an hourly worker who feared being told to hit the highway if he did not collude, but in another the dynamic is the same: I swapped my freedom for safety and security. I colluded.

Nothing will change until you and I recognize our dependency needs and our fears are part of what is going on in our inner life, and, like other inner life issues, they are in constant interplay with our outer work. These inner life issues were not created by the boss to whom we report or the organization for which we work, as much as we would like to blame them. "Nothing will change," Block says, "Until we can accept the fact that the fear we feel is our own creation. Granted, everyone feels it at some point, so it is culturally very common, but it is still ours" (2002, p. 109).

But when we face into and walk through our fears, summon enough courage to act authentically, and do it without blame or judgment, personal power accrues to us. When we name coercion as we experience it, and let others know we are calling the note, we accrue personal power. And when we call the note, we often find our fears were unfounded—we learn we can speak our truth to power without getting hit with a larger stick or having a carrot taken away.

The Alternative: Personal Power

Personal power is different from coercive power. Personal power comes from a different source. It is rooted in our authenticity and wholeness, not in a role or position. It is based on our competence and character and integrity. It accrues to us as we become our self, our true self, and when we engage in leadership as authentic and whole men and women. We are seen as being more powerful, not less, as we become vulnerable enough to acknowledge our gifts and limits, own that we cast shadow, and learn to say, "I don't know." We have power because of who we are more than for what we do.

There is yet another way that personal power is different from coercive power. Coercive power comes with a position in an organization or family or community; not everyone has it. But everyone has personal power. In the *Four-Fold Way,* a book that is dog-eared because I have read it so often, author and cultural anthropologist Angles Arrien says, "Many indigenous societies believe that we all possess 'original medicine': personal power duplicated nowhere else on the planet. No two individuals carry the same combination of talents and challenges" (1993, p. 21). While everyone can have personal power, power based on our talents and challenges, not everyone appears to know this or act on it. Even when I grant you personal power or authority—I acknowledge that you have original medicine—you may not believe you have it, or you may not claim it. Both verbs are important: I grant, you claim. And they may not always be in this order.

Our task is to discern and embrace the original medicine that is ours and that is duplicated nowhere else on the planet. As we embrace our personal power—and acknowledge gifts and challenges related to that power—we also identify the particular contributions we can make to the accomplishment of leadership tasks.

Here are several other differences in coercive and personal power: coercive power is "power over"; personal power is "power with." Coercive power can be used to force others to act in ways not in their self-interests or the best interest of the organization. Personal power is not used to force but is used to influence, to impact and to persuade; it is about showing up, having a position, and speaking our truth. Power is still an important dynamic in a relationship, but it is used differently and its use has different consequences—no more fight or flight by the other, no more need to commercialize commitment, no more ratcheting up the conflict through the use of bigger sticks or carrots. Here is a chart that describes the differences:

Coercive Power	*Personal Power*
Power based on sticks and carrots	Power based on integrity, authenticity, and character
Source is external to self	Source is internal to self
Can be given or taken away	Is granted and claimed
Position-centered	Person-centered
Used to control	Used to influence
Works when other is afraid or dependent	Works when other is respected and respectful
Based on fear	Based on love

There is a difference between claiming personal power and empowerment. In recent years empowerment has entered our lexicon and it suggests that one person—the manager, the boss, the principal, or the parent—shares his or her power with others, as in "she empowered him," or "he gave us the power to decide." The assumption underlying the language of empowerment is that power is a currency that can be given or taken away. But I have found that waiting to be empowered is like waiting for Santa Claus to come. It is waiting to be given a gift that cannot be gotten any other way. Authority to make a certain decision may be given, responsibility for certain tasks may be assigned, but personal power, I argue, cannot be given or taken away.

There is also a difference between empowering another person and granting them personal power or authority. When I grant you personal power I am not giving you something you do not have; I am acknowledging something that has accrued to you because of who you are. This is a subtle but important difference.

You and I act differently in our leadership roles and activities when we are granted, and have claimed, our personal power:

- We walk the talk. We are authentic and whole and trustworthy people, and who we are is reflected in what we do and how we act in our leadership roles. We are congruent and transparent. We lead with a deep sense of identity and integrity.
- We find our voice and use it. No more saying yes when we

want to say no; no more remaining silent when we think the team or organization is going in the wrong direction; no more hiding the values we cherish; no more agreeing with the boss in the public meeting only to criticize her afterwards. In other words, no more collusion.

- We are proactive, less reactive. No more waiting on the sidelines for someone else to send us into the game. Now we think of "leadership as everyone's vocation" and find appropriate ways to be involved. No more throwing verbal hand grenades at "them" for the stupid things they do after refusing their offer to have a seat at the table. Now we think of ourselves as having distinct gifts to offer to the accomplishment of leadership tasks and we offer them freely.

- We use our power (or our authority, if you prefer) to influence, to persuade, to have impact. We use our original medicine and power that has accrued to us to make a difference, hopefully a positive one. But we do not force or coerce or engage in "pay-for-play."

- We do not blame others for our internal realities. Blaming others for our fears, or insecurities, or dependency needs, is giving away our power; it says someone else is responsible and we are not. So, no more, "I did not speak my truth because he couldn't take it," or "I did not blow the whistle because around here they really do shoot the messenger," or even "He made me mad." Rather, the message might be, "I did not speak my truth because I was afraid." Even though it may not always true, it is better when we act as if we are 100 percent responsible for our thoughts and feelings. When we do, we embrace our personal power.

- We no longer swap freedom for safety and security, at least not without it being a conscious choice, a choice for which we accept full responsibility. This is not to say that there will not be times when we want someone or some organization to take care of us, to provide us a sense of safety, but even when we want this we know that it is an illusion, one that will not serve us well over the long haul.

- We assume responsibility and accountability for the whole

even when we don't have authority. No more waiting for change to start at the top. No more "we can't do it because they won't let us" before we have even tried. Peter Block calls the person who proactively assumes responsibility a citizen. "A citizen," he writes, "is one who is willing to be accountable for and committed to the well-being of the whole ... a citizen is one who produces the future, someone who does not wait, beg, or dream for the future" [2008, p. 63].

Power, Ego Self and True Self

There is often a very real arrogance associated with the use coercive power. It seems clear that I—or anyone—must feel some sense of superiority, some exaggerated sense of worth, to be willing to use a stick or carrot to force someone else to behave the way I want them to. And arrogance, I have learned, is what happens when healthy egos gets over-inflated, when self-confidence is taken to an extreme.

As noted earlier, healthy egos are a necessary strength that individuals must have if they are to contribute to the accomplishment of leadership tasks. We simply cannot be riddled with self-doubt and be effective. But when healthy egos become over-inflated, the asset becomes a liability.

Arrogance often has a surprising source: insecurity. I know this is true for me. The more insecure I am feeling, the more anxious I am about my place in the order of things, the more I want to have power over you. It is when I am insecure that I create one-up, one-down relationships. It is when I am not in touch with my own "original medicine" that I try to force you into behaving in certain ways. It is true for me; it was true for Milton, the executive I described at the beginning of this chapter; I suspect it is also true for you.

In contrast, individuals who engage in leadership tasks as their whole and authentic self have healthy, strong egos, know and embrace their personal power, and use it effectively to influence, persuade, advocate for, stand up to, represent the needs of the whole, and to serve the common good. And importantly, they have enough humility to know their gifts are not always sufficient, their insights are not always the keenest, their preferred decisions are not always right, and there is no "my way or the highway" in their practice of leadership. They invite others to share their gifts and skills and energies in the accomplishment of leadership tasks. These men and women are known for having self-confidence *and* humility.

Power and the Practices of Leadership

In the first chapter I described two practices of leadership: a traditional practice in which leadership is understood as the province of an extraordinary individual, and a second practice in which leadership is understood as the province of many ordinary men and women who offer their gifts and themselves to the accomplishment of leadership tasks. In the first practice leadership is embedded in a position—usually the person at the top of the organization or community pyramid—and in the second it emerges from the quality of interaction between and among people.

The first practice—what I call executive-as-leader—is alive and well in our culture, especially the culture of the United States. It is the dominant narrative. It is prevalent in business organizations, in school systems, in the church and other religious organizations, and in the communities in which we live. It is alive and well because it is what we think we want—leaders who are farsighted and bold, who can and will lead the parade, who have a clear sense of direction and the ability to articulate it in ways that excite us, and who offer us a sense of safety and security. Nothing is wrong with these desires, nothing except that they inevitably result in a one-up, one-down practice of leadership. A few are in the game while most are on the sidelines. The gifts of the few and not the many are valued. A few are accountable and responsible and the rest are not.

The traditional practice is patriarchal (or sometimes matriarchal), and we allow the patriarch to have enormous power over us. We pray he or she uses it wisely. It is not that we don't like strong, even dictatorial, leaders; the evidence is to the contrary. We like patriarchs and matriarchs—we elect them and support them—as long as they are benevolent. This usually means that they agree to protect us from harm and keep us safe. We like strong, dictatorial leaders because it gets us off the hook; they are responsible and we are not. When they turn out to be not so benevolent, we decide we elected the wrong person, or the board selected the wrong person, and we hope for a better outcome the next time.

Supporting patriarchy requires that we give away our power and allow others to have power over us. As I write this I am struck by how much power we have given away to the U.S. federal government in recent years, including giving up some cherished civil liberties, because we believe that these political patriarchs will take care of us. We allowed them to have power over us because we were afraid. We swapped freedom for safety and security, or at least this is the deal we thought we were making.

The use of coercive power in any shape or form will undermine the possibility of leadership being the province of many ordinary people working together. Collective leadership, relational leadership, or partnership—any of these names work for me—can only happen when the gifts, skills, energies, and personal power of many ordinary people are used to accomplish leadership tasks. Partnerships require real choice made by people who claim and use their personal power.

When we have claimed our personal power and decided to be partners, Peter Block says the question we need to ask is "what do we want to create together?" In *The Answer to How Is Yes*, Block writes:

> The question recognizes that we live in an interdependent world, that we create nothing alone. We may think we invented something, or achieved something on our own, but this belief blinds us to all that came before us and those who have supported us. It is a radical question, for it stabs at individualism, a cornerstone of our culture. It also declares that we will have to create or customize whatever we learn or whatever we import from others. Just having a conversation about this question brings people's deeper side into the room.... So many workplace conversations are about how we are going to deal with what *they* want to create. Question Six [this question] stops the political discourse about what *they* want from us and how we are going to respond and starts the purpose-filled discussion of what *we* will initiate. The dialogue alone levels the playing field, even if only for a moment [2002, p. 32].

We must change our basic assumption about power if it is to be used effectively in partnerships. As long as we think power is a limited resource, we will tend to hoard it. As long as we think it is in scarce supply, we will claim our power and try to deny others theirs. We protect our turf, withhold information, demarcate clear responsibilities and lines of authority, do all we can to keep others from playing in our sandbox. We hire or choose to work with others who are less powerful than we. In contrast, if we assume abundance, if we know power is not a limited resource, that it is part of the "original medicine" of all people and fed by all four of our energies; then our thinking about power, and our relationship to it, is changed. Interestingly, what we learn from experience is that we are granted more power by allowing others to claim and use theirs.

Leadership and Power: A Short Summary

Power is a dynamic that exists is every relationship.

There is a difference between coercive power and personal power.

Coercive power comes with a position, and is based on having sticks and carrots. Not everyone has it.

Personal power accrues to a person who is authentic and who authors his own life. Everyone has it, but not everyone knows or embraces it.

The more we become our self and act in our leadership roles out of a deep sense of wholeness and authenticity the more personal power we accrue.

There is a real and important difference between how coercive power and personal power are used in the accomplishment of leadership tasks. The former drains energy and life from people; the latter gives life and energy to them.

8. Organizations Worthy of the Soul

The XYZ Company (a pseudonym) is a major worldwide organization, well-known for the quality of its services and products. For the past several years I have been working with them in a leader development effort, and as part of this work we have explored the impact of their organizational culture on the behavior of the leaders—the men and women with whom I am working—and the impact of the leaders on the culture. The first step in this process is defining aspects of the XYZ culture. Here are a few of the ways they describe their culture:

- We are nice, nice to each other and nice to our clients. The good news is that we are collegial and collaborative. The bad news is that we are not always honest and we avoid conflict [in the language of this book, authenticity is not encouraged].
- We are data driven. We are adept at finding, understanding and using data. Because of our penchant for data and our ability to use it, we make good decisions. But there are times when the data will not point to a decision and at those times we often postpone decisions to search for more information. We are risk-averse.
- We favor tasks over people. We get the work done, deliver the quality work clients expect and deserve, and we do it in a timely way. This focus is reinforced in stories told throughout the organization. The downside is that our personal lives suffer and we burn out our people.
- We tend to be hierarchical. There is order and structure.

Employees are clear about direction, know what is expected of them, and we are a productive and profitable company. The downside of this normative way of doing leadership is that people at lower levels wait on direction from their superiors and do not claim their personal power to help shape the direction of their unit, group, or department.

As I work with the XYZ company and others like it, I ponder what type of organization is worthy of the soul, are safe places for whole and authentic men and women to make an appearance. I have asked, and am asking, all kinds of questions:

- What organizational cultures, structures, and systems encourage us to stay true to who we are, and help us keep who we are connected to what we do?
- What must happen in organizations for the men and women who work there to feel safe to be genuine and real and honest and vulnerable?
- What practice of leadership will encourage more of us to offer our gifts, skills, and energies?
- What is the metaphor for an organization that is worthy of the soul? If a well-oiled machine was what we thought we needed in the industrial era, what do we want or need today?
- How can we organize people and create structures so that work gets done *and* it calls forth the best we have within us?

Too often we—and I am one of the we—focus on leader development and leader formation without corresponding attention and focus on organization development, on the systems and structures in which the individual leader works. From many different work and life experiences I have learned it is not possible to separate the two. In my early work career I realized that I could not effectively work with and counsel youth unless I also tended to the family system of which they were apart. A few years later I joined the staff of a major corporation, and there I was in the leader development function while other colleagues were responsible for organization development. What I learned is that it did not work for me to help individuals learn to work in trust-based, cross-functional teams when the organization still rewarded individual performance. Organization development needed to work in parallel with individual leader development. For the past 12 years I have facilitated Courage to Lead retreats for those in serving professions—nonprofit leaders, educational leaders, clergy leaders, healthcare leaders, and attorneys. One overarching purpose of this work is to help individuals become and be themselves, and to root their leadership in their identity and integrity. Too often, after the retreats are over individuals return to organizations in which acting authentically is not encouraged or living and leading as whole persons is not promoted.

Here's what I have come to believe:

- We—you and I—yearn to find our way home individually, become and be authentic and whole, and we want to work in organizations that are life-giving and healthy, organizations that help us become the person we started out to be.
- Organizational structures and systems, corporate cultures and core values, and leadership practices either encourage or discourage true self from showing up. We wish for our organizations to be healthy and life-giving places for us to work and find meaning and purpose; if they are not all that healthy we wish for them to be benign; what we know is that some organizations are toxic, neither healthy nor benign. They do not have to be this way. We can create organizations worthy of the soul.
- Organizations influence our behavior but do not determine it. Even when organizational norms do not encourage authenticity and wholeness, we can decide to come out from hiding, be genuine and honest, find our voice and say "no" when we want to say "no," and speak our truth to power.
- Organizations can be successful *and* be healthy, life-giving places for people. It does not have to be either/or; it can be, and is, both/and.

The purpose of this chapter is to suggest things we can do so that organizations can be both/and: fulfill their mission *and* be places worthy of us doing soulful work.

We Can Shape the Organizational Culture

All organizations have a culture. Even the homeowners association where my wife and I live has a culture—there are typical ways we do things, things that grew out of our interactions more than anything we planned.

Culture is a set of informal norms that develop over time that prescribe particular and normative ways of being and doing. Culture is "the way we do things around here," and as the story about XYZ illustrates, the way we do things has an upside and downside, a pro and a con. Culture is never described in the standard operating procedure manual; it is never that clean and clear. Culture is sensed more than it can be observed—one organizational consultant I know says it is smelled more than measured. Culture is known by the stories that are told, stories that communicate, among other things, how decisions are made, what gets rewarded or punished, what are expected and acceptable behaviors (including dress and language), and that describe the self-image of the organization.

Stories both give shape to a culture and they can reinforce or recreate a culture. I have a good friend who once said to me, "In my company I am to do what I am told, and most of the times it means to color within the lines." He was not joking. I asked him how he learned that this was the expectation. He said, "These are the things you just learn while being part of the organization. No one tells you directly. Most of the time you just pick it up as you listen to the stories that are told. Or you do what I did: color outside the lines and get called into the principal's office." My friend was both describing one aspect of his company's culture, and as he told this story to others he was helping create or reinforce the culture. If the time comes when he can change his story he can help shape a different culture.

As I am writing the "bridgegate scandal" is making news in New Jersey. At this point, I do not know what Governor Christie knew about the bridge closing, if he knew anything at all, but I do wonder if the culture that was created in his office, and the stories that were told about what was expected and rewarded, encouraged behaviors that he now says are wrong. Stories told in any office help shape the culture; the culture influences employee's behaviors, and then stories about those behaviors either reinforce or recreate the culture. It is an on-going, cyclical process.

Because culture cannot be easily understood, much less quantified, it is not the first thing executives consider when thinking about changing or renewing their organization. Instead, executives tend to focus first on changing structures or people. Change the outer arrangement of people, or the people themselves, and transformation will happen. Move boxes around on the organizational chart and renewal will result. Add layers or reduce them, flatten the hierarchy or build it, move toward or away from leadership and management teams, centralize or decentralize, and positive change will result, or so the thinking seems to be. But seldom if ever does a change in the outer arrangements produce lasting and useful change in the culture of an organization.

A story makes this point well. A neighbor was for many years an executive in a large bank. He called his bank a "gentleman's club"—a highly successful gentleman's club, but not a place where confrontation and conflict were part of the culture—at least not open confrontation and conflict. Those who worked in this bank learned that the expected norm was to be "gentlemen." Several years ago this bank merged with a bank that had a very different culture—a bank in which individuals were more aggressive and hard-driving, more willing to take risks, more willing to surface differences. This cultural norm shaped the being and doing of its leaders. The back office aspects of merging the banks went reasonably well; it is relatively easy to change systems and structures. But merging or changing cultures was more difficult—it always is. There is no lever to pull to change it; it cannot be re-engineered like we think other parts of an organization can; it takes more than an act of will to merge two very different cultures. But slowly, as the different norms were identified and discussed, preferred norms were identified, reward systems were changed, and behavior also began to change. As behavior changed, stories that made the rounds also changed, and as stories changed a different culture evolved.

Several years ago I worked with a large chemical company that was merging two of its operating divisions. My work was to facilitate a team development experience for the new senior management team of the merged divisions. The executives of the parent company were wise enough to know the cultures of the two divisions were very different, and they recognized the merger would not finally be complete until the question of culture was addressed. But the members of the new senior management team did not want to go there; instead, they wanted to focus their time and energy on how to organize and manage the combined sales force and determine the appropriate headcount level for the newly merged division. These were important issues; each needed to be addressed. The cultural issues they wanted to keep on the back burner were also critical. One of the operating divisions was described to me as fast-paced and entrepreneurial, a "sexy" place to work, and one that paid scant attention to the few standard operating procedures they had. The other division was one of the oldest in the company, had long seen itself and had been seen as a cash cow, and in this division standard operating procedures were rules to be followed, not norms to be considered. The senior vice president of the newly merged divisions came from the "sexy" division.

During our work on the "hard stuff" I paid attention to the stories they told about what life was like in their former divisions. I listened for what behaviors were expected, which were honored, and which were punished. I listened for expectations for the right way for individuals to be and do. I listened for the informal norms that existed in each that drove decision-making.

As I paid attention to what was happening in the team development experience I noticed the different ways individuals from the two divisions treated authority figures. I witnessed the different ways they dealt with differences of opinion and managed conflict. I even took notes about the different language that was used by those from the different divisions.

When the time seemed to be right—and it was some time after we has started our work together—I offered my observations about what I had heard and seen. There was some denial and defensiveness, but there was more curiosity and interest. They were ready to engage in conversation about the differences in the cultures from which they came, and how those differences were already impacting the way they worked together. They were ready to be more intentional about creating a new and different culture.

The point is clear: attempts to change an organization without dealing with its culture will not produce lasting or useful results. And it will not create an organization worthy of an authentic and whole self making an appearance.

The good news is that culture is not static; it can and does change and evolve. You and I can help shape or recreate the culture of our civic group or company. As the stories I have told illustrate, culture is recreated as we tell new and different stories.

Not long ago I became aware of how the stories being told about a large church I know well are dramatically different than they were seven years ago; the change in culture had happened so slowly and so organically that it took me a long time to notice the full extent of it. Over these seven years the organization had gone from being inwardly- to outwardly-focused, from spending its time and energy maintaining itself to investing itself in its core mission. During this same time it added new programs, programs that would not have been acceptable, perhaps not even allowed, seven years earlier. It began partnerships with other like-minded organizations, partnerships that allowed it to expand and extend its outreach. Even the inner life of the organization changed; the organization now had a vibrant, full-of-life quality I had not experienced earlier. It went from being a cold organization to a warm one, from being wary to welcoming new ideas and new people, from doing things the way they had always been done to experimenting with new ways of doing ministry. Even the leadership narrative changed.

But it took seven years. The senior pastor of this church knew change was needed but he chose not to mandate it; in fact, he told me more than once that if the organization needed that kind of change agent he was not the person to do it. Instead, he thought of leadership as happening in a collective. Leadership began with the leadership team he created, and moved from there throughout the rest of the church. The minister convened the conversations. He asked the right questions. He kept ideas in front of the stakeholders. He provided important input. He felt a sense of urgency, and communicated it effectively, but he did not allow a sense of false urgency to infect the organic process. He knew his gifts and acknowledged his limits. He was clear that the cultural change would happen only if it emerged from the interaction of all the stakeholders.

When I first joined the faculty at the Center for Creative Leadership it was an organization of some 80 people, all located in the headquarters in Greensboro, North Carolina. We were a chaotic organization—we had order and chaos. We did not want to be too tightly organized. We had few standard operating procedures, no job descriptions, and very little hierarchy.

One of my favorite stories from the early days at CCL is that employees used to gather after lunch to play volleyball on the back lawn. Meaning to be helpful, a manager put lines on the volleyball court. People quit playing. The stories told about this were more important that the event itself; the stories helped shape CCL's culture. We want employees, I was told, "who play outside the lines." Any attempt to put too many systems or structures in place became the fodder for someone saying, "they are putting lines on the volleyball court." My colleagues and I liked the culture we had and did not want it to change, at least not in any dramatic way.

But as CCL got older and larger, the culture did change. More systems and structures were put in place. More lines were drawn on the volleyball court. We started hiring individuals who wanted to play inside the lines. Most importantly, different stories were told about what was important, what behaviors were acceptable, and what formal and informal norms were now a part of the operating instructions. As the stories changed the culture changed.

As I have worked with organizations like XYZ, listened to my friend's story, read about "bridgegate," and been an active participant in other stories, it has become clear into me that we shape culture and culture shapes us. In some cultures we are encouraged us to be real and authentic, in others we learn it is safer and saner to go into hiding. Some cultures reinforce nice; others support honesty and candor. Some cultures reward those who act with a deep sense of integrity; in others a wink and nod are given to integrity while what's rewarded is doing whatever it takes to get new clients or maintain present ones. Some cultures are healthy places for the soul to make an appearance, some are not.

The important reality is that cultures can and do change. Slowly and over time, culture changes. Change the norms, change the stories told, change the leadership narrative, and culture changes. Intentionally or unwittingly, you and I either contribute to the change and transformation of our organization's culture, or we reinforce the one we have. But we have a choice: we can help shape the culture so that is more life-giving and healthy, rather than being victimized by it.

Today we need to think of ourselves as creators of culture rather than passive recipients of it.

We Can Learn to Orbit the Giant Hairball

When our attempts to shape the culture of our organization—or our group or department in a larger organization—do not work, we have at least one more option: we can orbit the giant hairball.

I borrow this phrase from Gordon MacKenzie, who wrote a book with a similar name, *Orbiting the Giant Hairball, A Corporate Fool's Guide to Surviving with Grace.* MacKenzie wrote the book after a thirty-year career with Hallmark Cards, where his job was to be creative. So what's a giant hairball? It is a metaphor for an organization reality that one policy—or one hair—keeps getting added on to another until there is a giant hairball. MacKenzie writes:

> Every new policy is another hair for the Hairball. Hairs never get taken away, only added. Even frequents reorganizations have failed to remove hairs (people, sometimes; hairs, never). Quite the contrary, every reorganization seems to add a whole new layer of hairs ... with the increase in the Hairball's mass comes a corresponding increase in the Hairball's gravity. There is such a thing as corporate gravity. *The gravitational pull a body exerts increases as the mass of that body increases.* And like physical gravity, it is the nature of corporate gravity to suck everything into its mass—in this case, into the mass of Corporate Normalcy [1996, p. 31, italics in original].

MacKenzie goes on to note that many a "Hallmarker" succumbed to the pull of this relentless gravity. Others escaped to other endeavors to avoid the gravitational pull of the Hallmark hairball, only to find that their new organization had an even larger hairball. Yet others at Hallmark found a way to orbit the Hallmark Hairball, maintain their relevance and creativity, remain true to themselves, and stay engaged in helping Hallmark fulfill its mission.

I have seen the corporate hairball get larger in many different organizations. As organizations get larger and older they also tend to become more closed and less open; the standard operating procedure manual grows larger, never smaller; bureaucracy grows, never shrinks; and individuals are expected to conform to "corporate normalcy," however it is defined. The organization says something to the employee like: these are our policies, our procedures, our cultural norms, our systems— learn to fit in by conforming. The problem, of course, is that corporate normalcy does not recognize that each of us is a distinctive combination of gifts and limits, strengths and weaknesses, different temperaments, and that each of us has particular gifts and energies to offer to the accomplishment of leadership tasks and the work of the organization. The goal of corporate normalcy is not to help each of us become the person we started out to be, but instead to help us fit the corporate mold. Giant hairballs and organizations worthy of the soul cannot easily coexist.

Like MacKenzie, I have seen what happens when individuals succumb to the gravitational pull of the hairball. When people get sucked into the hairball they lose that which makes them original and distinctive; they lose their core self and become another organizational person; they may still be a false self or ego self—and these often fit with corporate normalcy, but they lose sight of their true self. True self gets entombed in the bureaucracy. But when individuals get outside the orbit they lose their relevance. They are sidelined, sometimes fired, but often just ignored. They live in their own world, sometimes proudly, occasionally defiantly, but they are no longer contributing to the organizational mission.

Marshall was one of the most gifted and creative thinkers I have known. He thought outside the box, challenged prevailing assumptions about leadership, and asked provocative and important questions. Marshall was a unique person, a distinctive combination of "gifts, skills, and energies." He made lasting contributions to the work of the organization, contributions that put our organization on the map and built its reputation. But he disdained the "mass of corporate normalcy." He detested the "creeping bureaucracy" he saw in the organization, and encouraged others to do the same. He hated organizational politics and refused to play. He paid little attention to the standard operating procedures, especially the ones that made no sense to him. He simply and only wanted to do the work that was his to do, and make the contribution that was his to make. But he also did not learn to orbit the hairball and, in fact, he flew so far outside the orbit he was eventually asked to leave.

So what does it take to orbit the giant hairball? Mackenzie says it is this:

> If you are interested (and it is not for everyone), you can achieve Orbit by finding the personal courage to be genuine and to take the best course of action to get the job done rather than follow the pallid course of corporate appropriateness ... to be of optimum value you must invest

enough individuality to counteract the pull of Corporate Gravity, but not so much that you escape that pull altogether. Just enough to stay out of the hairball … through this measured assertion of your own uniqueness, it is possible to establish a dynamic relationship with the hairball [1996, p. 31].

Find courage. Be genuine. Invest enough individuality. These words and phrases fit with the theme of this book: be whole and authentic men and women; become the person you started out to be; find your way home, home to true self; and be true self rather than allowing yourself to get sucked into the "mass of corporate normalcy." This is not easy. The gravitational pull of the hairball is strong. Others will expect you to conform, to become and be who they and the corporation wants you to be. But you can do it. It requires paying attention. And courage.

We Can Define and Act on Core Values

In 1995, James O'Toole, then vice president at the Aspen Institute, wrote, "Today's corporate executives believe they are struggling with an unprecedented leadership challenge to *create internal strategic unity within a chaotic external environment.* That is, they are convinced that today's leaders must create **strong, shared corporate values** to unite their increasingly decentralized operations" (1995, xiii, words in bold mine). A little later in the introduction to *Leading Change,* O'Toole wrote, "…trust emanates from leadership based on shared purpose, shared vision and shared values" (1995, xiii).

In the first chapter I wrote that one of the leadership tasks was to create a shared vision or shared direction for the organization. Now I add another task: the development of shared core values.

Shared values mean that the core values are co-created through a process that is inclusive and allows broad participation. Values cannot be imposed or commanded. Years ago I learned from Sid Simon, then a professor at the University of Massachusetts, that values, by definition, must be chosen freely, chosen from among alternatives, and chosen with full acceptance of the consequences. And, Simon suggested, values are things we not only say we cherish and prize but that we act on, and act on repeatedly.

Core values are different than aspirational values. Aspirational values are ideals we wish we were or wish we could attain, but core values are those things we say we cherish and prize *and* act on now. This difference is important. When an organization says it values straight talk and candor, but the reality is that confrontation and conflict are avoided, candor maybe an aspirational value but the core value is being nice or friendly or cooperative. When an organization says it values individuality but actually expects everyone to succumb to the "mass of corporate normalcy," individuality is not a core value. When organizations say they value diversity, but women are paid less than men, and there are no people of color in the C-suite, and those past age 62 are deemed too old to contribute, diversity may be an aspirational value but it is not a core value. Nothing wrong with aspirational values, per se. They may even point organizations and people in them in a healthy direction. But it is the right kind of core values that help create healthy and life-giving organizations, organizations that encourage individuals to become and be themselves.

Recently I saw the difference in core and aspirational values play out in Looking Glass, a realistic simulation of a fictitious business, including one day in the life of a manager/leader. I saw this difference while serving on the faculty of a leadership development program in a large and well-known American company, in which Looking Glass was a major component. In short, a plant manager in a foreign country knew if he paid a "bribe" to a government official he could free up production in his plant and use that production to sell more glass and create a much larger profit for the company. The plant manager was clearly uncomfortable paying the bribe but his boss argued that paying bribes was a standard way of doing business in the country, that Looking Glass need to be flexible and respond to different business practices in different countries and cultures, and he encouraged the plant manager to "keep it quiet and pay it." The core value? Do whatever it takes to increase profits.

To identify the core values of an organization pay less attention to what is printed on the plexiglass and posted in every conference room and more attention to who and what gets rewarded and punished. Listen and learn from how success is defined, what is required to be promoted or be given plum assignments, and how "corporate normalcy" is described. Even more, pay attention to the behaviors you reward and those you punish, to whom you give the most interesting work, and how you reinforce "corporate normalcy." Here again, you can create shared core values—life-giving values—in your part of the organization, and you do not have to wait on anyone else to give you permission before you do.

In the previous quote by O'Toole, he named one of the core values that is needed: trust. We cannot create organization worthy of the soul if *trust* is not a core value. If I do not trust that my distinctive combinations of "gifts, skills, and energies" will be honored, I will be less likely to use them. When I do not trust that my voice will be heard, I will be less likely to use it. When I do not trust that honesty will be appreciated, but in fact the messenger does get shot, I am less likely to speak my truth to power. When I do not trust that when I am open and vulnerable confidentiality will be maintained, I am more likely to stay in hiding. There are many other core values that individuals in a group or department of organization may share, many others that make the smaller unit or larger organization worthy of the soul, but trust is a good place to start.

We Can Change the Leadership Culture

Different practices of leadership were described in the first chapter. I mention them again here because changing leadership culture and leadership practices is one of the most important things we can do to create organizations in which true self (or core self or soul) will show up. Some practices of leadership are dispiriting; they drain the life and energy out of people; they do not allow all individuals to contribute their gifts, skills, and energies to the accomplishment of leadership tasks; they send the soul into hiding. Other practices of leadership are inspiriting and life-giving; they allow broad participation in leadership processes, and they provide a safer place for the soul to appear.

In 2009, four colleagues from CCL wrote a paper on transforming leadership cultures (McGuire et al., 2009). Three beliefs, all research-based, shaped their recommendations: (1) culture can be transformed; (2) companies (and organizations of all types) have no choice but to change; and (3) choosing the right leadership culture is the difference between success and failure in an organization. The authors then described three distinct leadership cultures:

> **Dependent** leadership cultures hold that only people in positions of authority are responsible for leadership.
> **Independent** leadership cultures assume that leadership emerges as needed from a variety of individuals based on knowledge and expertise.
> **Interdependent** leadership cultures view leadership as a collective activity that requires mutual inquiry, learning and a capacity to deal with complex challenges [2009, p. 8].

The authors go on to suggest we transform our leadership culture by recognizing what leadership culture is presently being used in our organization, and then determining what culture is needed to meet current challenges and opportunities. They argue the more complex the challenge and the higher the need for innovation, the greater the need for an interdependent culture.

I call the dependent culture the executive-as-leader practice of leadership, and I describe the interdependent culture as partnership. As I wrote earlier, in today's world we often need leadership tasks to be accomplished by a collective—in partnerships—more than by a single extraordinary individual. The challenges organizations face require this approach.

There is another reason, a more important reason, to move toward a different leadership culture. Leadership-as-partnership (or collective leadership or shared leadership) is based on the belief that leadership is everyone's vocation and that every individual has something, "gifts, skills, and energies" to offer to the accomplishment of leadership tasks. Partnerships honor the distinctive contributions of the many. In partnership there is no one-up or one-down, but instead everyone works together for the benefit of the whole. Partnerships work when every individual finds his or her voice, speaks truth, says "no" when there is disagreement with a direction discussed or strategy planned, and engages as a whole and authentic person.

In contrast, autocratic, top-down leadership, especially when it is accompanied by the use of coercive power, is demeaning and dispiriting. Autocratic leaders often get compliance, but seldom get commitment. As the name suggests, this practice of leadership often causes "followers" to be dependent, to wait on direction, to take few risks, and to do what they are told. It is not a practice of leadership worthy of the soul.

We can change the leadership culture in our small corner of the larger organization—our work group, our department, our division—even if the whole organization is not ready to change. The "we can't do it because they won't let us" is a stale excuse. It is being done, and we can do it. We can act as partners to set direction, build alignment, maintain commitment and navigate the whitewater of change. We can work together to create a leadership culture that is effective, productive and worthy of the soul.

We Can Adopt and Use Natural Metaphors for Our Organizations

In chapter two I suggested that nature offers the best metaphor for understanding individual formation. Like nature, our lives go through seasons, times of renewal and times of decay, times of abundance and times of drought, times of dormancy and times of new growth. Using nature as a metaphor, we understand there is no end-point to the process of our formation. Becoming and being true self is not an end to be achieved; it is not a destination, but a life-long journey. What's more, the metaphor of nature lets us know we cannot make things happen; we cannot make of ourselves whatever we want to be. If we were able to do so, I would have been a famous catcher for the New York Yankees, a latter-day version of Yogi Berra. We are gardeners of our lives, not mechanics.

Nature is also the best metaphor for understanding organizations. It is not a metaphor we often use. Rather, we still think of organizations as machines. We want them to be well-oiled. Organizations are engineered, or reengineered, to improve efficiency and speed, and increase size. Structures are changed, and people put in different boxes on a chart (that's a life-giving notion, isn't it?), because of an assumption that there are levers we can pull that will produce the results we want. Employees are seen as interchangeable parts; at least that is the perception and often the goal.

When organizations are seen as machines the answer to "how to change or renew?" is obvious. Improve an organization like you would improve a product. To get a better output start with the right input, and

152

then make sure that the right quality control mechanisms are in place to eliminate failures and mistakes. With the right processes in place, the organization will, just like its products, keep getting better and better. It is called continuous improvement. The goal is stability, control, and zero defects—a perfect organization. It seems so rational.

Thinking of organizations as machines and trying to renew them through the right engineering interventions might improve productivity, increase efficiency, or get things up to speed more quickly. It might also allow the organization to exert better control on outcomes, or behave a bit more predictably. This is not renewal, however, and it does not create an organization worthy of the soul.

Margaret Wheatley says the same thing this way:

> The accumulating failures at organizational change can be traced to a fundamental but mistaken assumption that organizations are machines. Organization-as-machines is a seventeenth century notion from a time when philosophers began to describe the universe as a great clock. Our modern belief in prediction and control originated in these clockwork images. Cause and effect were simple relationships. Everything could be known. Organizations and people could be engineered into efficient solutions. Three hundred years later, we still search for "tools and techniques" and "change levers"; we attempt to "drive" change through our organizations; we want to "build" solutions and "reengineer" for peak efficiency.... [But] these days, a different ideal for organizations is surfacing. We want organizations to be adaptive, flexible, self-renewing, resilient, learning, and intelligent—attributes found only in living systems. The tension of our time is that we want our organizations to be *living systems*, but we only know how to treat them as machines [2005, p. 32].

This is the new metaphor that is needed for new times. Instead of a well-oiled machine, we need to think of organizations as living systems.

Nature offers a reliable and trustworthy metaphor for understanding how living systems work. Consider oak trees in a forest, for example. In one season of the year the trees shed their leaves so that there is room for new growth later on. They let go of their leaves as part of an on-going cyclical process. They don't always let go easily, but they let go. In contrast, we create "sunset laws" to force ourselves to do what oak trees do naturally. In some cases, we refuse to let go; instead we keep trying to do more and more at greater speed and efficiency. We do not realize that one of the most important strategic questions we can ask is what to stop doing.

Then the trees enter a time of dormancy, a time when no growth is apparent on the surface but a time when roots are digging deep into sustaining soil. It is not quarter-to-quarter growth and production for trees. No one has found a way to engineer them so that they produce acorns year-round.

After the dark cold days of winter, trees in early spring begin to show signs of new life. New buds appear, not from a carefully planned and implemented new product development effort, but from a messy and chaotic process. Then for the trees there are times of great abundance, though, as sometimes happens, there may be times of drought. Times of abundance are where we would like to stay in our organizational life—sales and profits are up, morale is good, things are humming. But it does not always continue this way, not for the trees and not for us. The seasons begin again and the cycle continues; change is continuous, and organizations, like the trees, need to be flexible and resilient enough to adapt.

One of the reasons trees thrive is that they are part of a larger ecosystem. They do not make it on their own. They do not survive without sun and rain, without other trees providing protection from harsh and hard winds, and without the nourishment they receive from the decaying matter of other plant life. Oak trees have a lot to teach us about the interdependence of life.

There is another important lesson that oak trees have to offer us: change is not an intrusion. It is not like an unwelcome guest who shows up at the doorstep hoping to stay a while. For an oak tree, like for other living systems, change is the norm, an organizing principle.

In *Crises and Renewal*, David Hurst and his colleague, Brenda Zimmerman, use the ecosystem of a forest—another living system—as a metaphor for organizations. They suggest that ecosystems go through four phases. They write, "the phases of growth, conservation, destruction and renewal ... are widely observed tendencies of natural systems" (2002, p. 98). These four phases parallel the cycle of the oak tree just described. This is what we can expect from living systems. The four phases appear linear, but in truth they are part of one on-going cycle. There are no clear boundaries between them. Forests do not go through the phases with clear and certain timing. Hurst and Zimmerman also note that change is continuous, that "at any given moment there will be some parts of the forest in every phase of the ecocycle" and that "renewal requires destruction ... the only way to open up spaces in the forest is to creatively destroy the larger-scale structures that hog the resources" (2002, p. 102).

The Composite Corporation, a company I described in some detail in my last book, is a good example of an organization as a living system. I began my work with it during its early growth stage. It was a time of experimentation, of learning by trial and error, of designing new products, and starting new research. Creativity and innovation flourished; thinking outside the box was encouraged. New ideas were welcome. There was little bureaucracy, few organizational systems, and no standard operating procedures manual.

Composite became successful. Research was published that built Composite's reputation. There was a waiting list for the purchase of its flagship products. New staff came on board. During this time Composite entered the conservation phase. Products that paid off were expanded; those that did not were dropped. In general, new products were imitations of previous and successful ones rather that ground-breaking new ones. New offices were opened with the express intent of developing new products for new markets. It was a good idea, but before new products got a chance to take root, the decision was made to imitate what was already working. There was not as much self-organization; now structure was planned and imposed.

To be sure, not all parts of Composite were in the conservation phase during this time. There were "open patches" in the organization where new ideas flourished, new products were developed and older products were revised, new services were offered to clients, and investments were made in new and uncertain ideas. The boundaries between the growth phase and the conservation phase at Composite were not clear and distinct.

Today Composite is in the growth *and* conservation phase. New offices are being opened around the globe and conserving the best of what has been created and produced still drives the organization. New products are being developed and old ones are still being imitated. New research is being done and old research is being replicated. New knowledge is being generated and the organization clings to and uses knowledge generated years ago.

For a living system such as Composite the necessary next phase is destruction. Hurst calls it "creative destruction" because the destruction makes it possible for renewal to happen. He suggests the option for organizational leaders is to have a "planned burn" that clears away not just the underbrush but also some mature trees to avoid a forest fire that is much harder to control. The idea that any living system needs planned burns is a hard notion to fathom, especially for those inside an organization.

I have worked for and with organizations in which some individuals knew it was time for a planned burn. They understood at a deep level that their current organizational structures and systems no longer made sense and were, in fact, suffocating the organization and its people. Deciding to clear away the underbrush is a hard decision to make. Government organizations fail at this, religious organizations try it and give up, and business organizations usually have a successful planned burn only when external forces require it. For those of us looking in from the outside it is easy to say that an organization, like a forest, needs to go through a time of crises or destruction if it is to be renewed, but for individuals on the inside the fear is that a planned burn may scorch them. But remember, the choice is a planned burn or a forest fire.

A planned burn describes what happened to America's big three automobile manufacturers several years ago. For years the strategy had been to invest in larger, gas-guzzling trucks and SUVs; it is a strategy that once seemed rational but, in hindsight, now seems short-sighted. Sales plummeted—partly due to the economy but partly because the companies were producing cars Americans did not want to buy. The cost required to build each car or truck was too high, especially when compared to foreign competitors. The companies were hemorrhaging money. The debate in Congress was about whether providing bailout money would help the big three automakers survive or if it would be simply throwing good money after bad. With or without the bailout money, the choice facing the automakers was stark and clear: renew or die. The three automobile companies each chose a "planned burn"— shut down plants and car lines, sell assets, lay off workers, and reduce other costs.

Why not have the same urgency to renew, the same compelling need to create a different future, before a crisis occurred? Inertia and complacency set in. Momentum carries the organization. Hubris is often a companion to success. Those who run organizations assume that success requires continuing to do what has always been done, and executives and managers get trapped by their habits. It is hard for organizations to renew themselves, to even consider the need for renewal, when things are going well. As with individuals, crises are often a necessary catalyst for organizational renewal.

But when we understand organizations as living systems, we also know that crisis and renewal are companions, that renewal is not an intrusion but another aspect to an on-going process, that every organization lives in and is dependent on a larger ecosystem, and that growth and renewal are organic processes. When we adopt a natural metaphor, when we see our organizations as living systems, we can begin to imagine ways of being and working together that are worthy of the soul.

We Can Pay Attention to Organizational Structure

Most organizational charts I see these days still have people in boxes, with lines that define reporting relationships, and other lines that connect roles. These organizational charts make everything look so clean and precise, so orderly. They define silos more than they provide a holistic view of organizations. They look more mechanical than organic, and they certainly do not represent a living system.

If you look at typical organization charts, it is easy to think hierarchies are still important to getting the core work of the organization accomplished. Before technology flattened organizations and made it possible for anyone to be in touch with anyone else without using the hierarchy, this was how some organizations worked. When I joined the staff of a corporation in the late 1970s this is how we got much of our work accomplished: messages or requests were sent up, across, and then down the organization, and the person on the receiving end followed the same process in responding. And in those days managers got their work done through those who reported directly to them; this was, in fact, the definition of management work. But this is no longer the reality.

Today the nature of organizations, the way work gets accomplished, and the role of the manager/leader have changed. More organizations these days are what Dee Hock, founder and former CEO of VISA, calls chaordic—a combination of chaos and order. Chaordic organizations are living systems that blend order and chaos, and in doing so they demonstrate some of the same organizing principles as nature. It is hard to capture a living system like a chaordic organization on an organizational chart.

The way work gets done and agendas are accomplished in organizations has also changed. Today organizational leaders know much of the work of the organization can be done more effectively by cross-functional teams, and these leaders are trying to breakdown silos and create more collaborative and cooperative ways of working together. To do this, they know they must create new systems and structures. The old organization chart with people in boxes does not reflect this new reality.

And the work of the manager/leader has changed. No longer does the manager/leader get work done only through the people who report directly to her; now she must get tasks accomplished through a vast array of people, most of whom do not report to her. Chris Ernst and Donna Chrobot-Mason published *Boundary Spanning Leadership*, which defines the five boundaries individuals must bridge if they are to get their agenda accomplished: vertical, horizontal, stakeholder, geographic, and demographic. The fact that these boundaries must be spanned adds chaos to what might otherwise be an orderly process.

What's the structure of a chaordic organization or a living system? What is the organizing principle? How might it be drawn and put on paper? New organizational forms and structures are emerging, but right now there are more questions than answers, and more hopes than actual structures to propose.

My hopes are that the new organization will be more fluid and dynamic than static; more chaordic than clean and neat; that it will be a living system rather than an engineered attempt to put people in the right box. I hope what we design will replace hierarchies with interrelated networks; the new structure or form will encourage openness and inclusiveness and participation in the leadership process; and the organizational form will allow the organization to deal with the adaptive challenges it faces, those challenges that cannot be solved by a single authoritative leader.

The structure I can now imagine is a collection of interlocking or connected circles, circles that change as some tasks are accomplished and other emerge, circles that change as membership changes, or as new directions or new strategies are set. And, by now you know I think leadership is everyone's vocation; I imagine leadership tasks will be accomplished in the circles in an open and participatory way.

There is one thing I cannot imagine: putting people in boxes.

A Brief Summary

Organizations are not always worthy of the soul, but they can be. It is what we want and deserve.

We—all of us—can help create organizations worthy of the soul by tending to the culture we are growing, by helping define and act on core values, and by helping define new and more appropriate systems and structures.

We can change the leadership culture in our corner of the organization even if the larger organization is not ready, and in this process we need to see ourselves as gardeners, not mechanics.

We can create and act on shared core values, values that honor and respect the distinctive contribution individuals are ready to offer to the accomplishment of leadership tasks, and values that support wholeness and authenticity.

We can encourage and support new ways of organizing to accomplish work. Included in this is being intentional about thinking of organizations as living systems, designing structures and forms that support living systems, and being willing to live with the chaos that is always part of living systems.

9. *Embracing Paradoxes*

I don't like paradoxes. I identify with what poet Gunilla Norris says, "Our minds do not like paradoxes." I have always liked clarity and certainty and, I confess, when I have achieved both I feel safe and secure. Conversely, when there is too much ambiguity, I feel unsafe.

Along the way I learned another truth, also named by Norris in the same poem, "We each possess a deeper level of being, however, which loves paradox." This is true for me. These days I love living into the fullness of a paradox and seeing a deeper truth than what appears on the surface to be a contradiction.

This is clearly a paradox: I don't like paradoxes; I love paradoxes.

As I was writing the earlier chapters of this book, and reflecting on my journey, I realized that in the process of becoming a whole and authentic person, and engaging in leadership from that place, there are paradoxes I needed to embrace. I assume the same is true for you.

In this chapter I suggest some of the paradoxes we must embrace on our journey to true self and authentic leadership. It provides a summary of the road we have traveled and offers new perspectives on life and leadership.

Organizational Paradoxes

Organizations must experience destruction if they are to be renewed. I started thinking about this paradox during the time that David Hurst spent a year at the Center for Creative Leadership writing his and Zimmerman's book, *Crises and Renewal.* I remember well Hurst's colloquium when he described the four stages in the life cycle of ecosystems and organizations: early growth, conservation (conserving what works best), destruction, and renewal. The first two phases did not surprise me; the third one did. I remember asking myself that day if there wasn't a way to renew an organization without it going through the painful process of destruction. Hurst's answer was simple: "no." He likened the renewal of an organization to the renewal of a forest; he said that day, and later wrote: "renewal requires destruction. The only way to open up spaces in the forest is to creatively destroy large-scale structures that hog the resources" (p. 102). The idea that renewal requires destruction is a difficult paradox to understand much less embrace; at least it is for me.

I thought more deeply about this paradox as I got to know Jim Harnish and read his book, *You Only Have to Die*. It is the story about the renewal of Hyde Park United Methodist Church in Tampa, Florida, where Harnish then served as senior pastor. When he was appointed to Hyde Park in 1992, it had been in existence at the same location for 93 years. The church was "clear about its past, somewhat foggy about its present, and didn't have a clue about its future" (p. 40). Hyde Park had moved beyond the life cycle stages of growth and conservation, and was in a time of decay if not destruction. Harnish wrote, "The changes in store for us involved more than just tinkering around the edges of our life together. That would have done as much good as rearranging the deck chairs on the *Titanic....* It would, in fact, involve the possibility of death—at least the death of some old assumptions and attitudes so that new things might come to life" (p. 24).

Here's the important paradox: as organizations embrace death and destruction, understand it as necessary and not bad, they are renewed. Whether it is the death of an attitude or set of assumptions, the death of a program or product, the loss of a huge part of the business, or as in the case of Hyde Park, the loss of a significant number of members, the other side of death is renewal.

Organizations, like all living systems, need both chaos and order if they are to thrive. I like order; I don't like chaos. I spent a lot of years thinking, or at least hoping, that my life and work in organizations could be planned, and then carried out in an orderly, sequential way—my mantra was plan the work and work the plan. During the time I worked for a major oil and gas company, we introduced and taught supervisors and managers a planning process that was linear and sequential, just what I thought was needed. Before setting budgets in the fall of each year managers set goals for what would be done in the coming year, decide how the what would be accomplished, make sure they knew who would do the what, and then propose the budget needed to insure the what got done. It was clean and neat and orderly. I liked it. It didn't work.

It didn't work because as soon as the new year started, a change in the price of a barrel of oil, the discovery of a new oil field, evidence that an old field was declining more quickly than anticipated, or the selection of a new president—to name but four of many possibilities—would mean that the goals set three months prior were no longer relevant or a priority.

But we—those of us in management positions—did not give up on the idea that planning should be linear and sequential. We only decided that we might need several iterations of it in a given year. So we created and used mid-year reviews. Goals, strategies and objectives were revised, and new budgets to support them were created and approved. We did not want to live with the chaos; we wanted order. When the planning process did not produce order we felt like we had failed.

The planning process was but one of the ways we tried to avoid chaos and impose order in this company. We created organizational charts that delineated a clear chain of command that, among other things, let individuals know who they could and could not talk to. The result was that often communication went up, and across, and back down the organization rather than going straight across. We used position levels to determine what size office an individual could have, what and how many pictures could be put on the wall, what floor covering the office could have, even what color the office would be. I remember the time a new colleague decided to come in the weekend before she started to paint her office a different color, one more pleasing to her. By the end of her first day it had been repainted the standard office gray. We assumed that allowing individuals these choices would have ushered in chaos, or at least disorder. We provided individuals detailed job descriptions and a place in a clear, black box on an organizational chart to keep roles and responsibilities clean and clear. In this organization I was a "specialist," a training and development specialist, and it was important that I knew and remembered the difference in my responsibilities and those of the employee relations generalist. It would maintain order. It would prevent chaos. At the time it made sense to me.

It no longer does. I left the oil and gas company and joined the faculty at the Center for Creative Leadership (CCL) in 1984 and found an organization that then did not operate with a strong chain of command, did not have tightly defined job descriptions, and did not attempt to "box" employees in. Early on I remember trying hard to get clear about my role in relation to a colleague—I like order, remember—and when she and I could not agree, we went together to our boss to get him to define our responsibilities for us. He refused. He believed chaos and creativity were linked, and that new ways for her and I to creatively work together would emerge from the chaos I did not like. I was surprised, even a bit chagrined, by his attitude. I have since learned he was right. Out of order and chaos our relationship began to thrive.

Order and chaos can also be observed in an organization's planning process. I have learned, somewhat slowly, the linear and sequential planning processes I liked don't usually work and those that combine order and chaos usually do. I learned this as I noticed that organizational strategies are unplanned as much if not more than they are planned, and that the actual strategy of an organization is a blend of intentional and emergent strategy, which is, of course, a combination of order and disorder.

I have seen this blending of intentional and emergent strategy work in two different ways. One organization for which I consulted had an annual planning cycle—they set goals and strategies and objectives—but they stayed nimble enough to take advantage of new opportunities when they arose. They did not expect order to prevail throughout the year; they were opportunistic and welcomed the emergence of new strategic possibilities. In another organization, the leadership team spent time and energy getting crystal-clear about its mission and its purpose, but they did not set strategies—they waited for strategic opportunities to emerge as they went through the year. The mission statement provided them a sense of order; because it was so clear it made it much easier to decide which new opportunities they would embrace and which they wouldn't. In each organization order and chaos were not seen as oppositional; they were embraced as paradox.

But there is a far deeper level in which order and chaos are at work in organizations. Meg Wheatley described this reality in, *Leadership and the New Science.* She wrote:

> We have even found order in the event that epitomizes total disorder—chaos ... chaos theory shows, if we look at a system long enough and with the perspective of time, it always demonstrates its inherent orderliness ... throughout the universe, then, order exists within disorder and disorder within order.... Linear thinking demands that we see things as separate states: One needs to be normal, the other exceptional. Yet there is a way to see this ballet of chaos and order, of change and stability, as two complementary aspects in the process of growth, neither of which is primary [1992, pp. 20, 21].

It does not serve us and our organizations well to think of order and chaos as separate states, and to think of order as the preferred norm. For organizations to thrive, order and chaos must be understood as a paradox to be held.

Substantive organizational change and renewal takes time and must be approached with a sense of urgency. In the last chapter I wrote that organizational change takes patience. I told a story of how the leadership team of a large church spent seven years changing their organizational culture. The team did it thoughtfully and one step at a time, but it was always on the front burner. The organizational leaders—and there were many—kept their shoulders to the flywheel and kept moving forward. They were always proactive. They learned that renewing an organization is akin to turning around the Queen Mary—it requires slow and steady work.

Paradoxically, substantive change and renewal also requires a sense of urgency. John Kotter, a professor emeritus at Harvard and a leading expert on leadership and change, says it this way, "At the very beginning of any effort to make change of any magnitude, if a sense of urgency is not high enough and complacency is not low enough, everything else becomes much more difficult" (2008, p. ix).

Kotter goes on to distinguish between a necessary sense of urgency and a false sense of urgency. Maintaining a frenetic pace of activity, creating one task force after another to study a new opportunity or decide how to respond to a hazard, or making elaborate Power Point presentations to detail a proposal, is confusing a false sense of urgency with genuine urgency. Real urgency is marked by moving forward, making decisions, taking action and looking for small wins. The leadership team that took seven years to change the culture of their church organization was always moving forward, sometimes taking only small steps, but making decisions and taking action nonetheless. They acted slowly, but with urgency.

Complacency is the enemy of urgency. Complacency usually appears in what David Hurst calls the conservation phase of an organization's life cycle. After an initial growth phase, organizations begin conserving the best of what is. They adapt current products rather than develop new ones; they invest only in products or programs that are certain to be successful; they don't seek out new opportunities in the marketplace; and they ignore warning signs or hazards. It is precisely because of complacency that the third phase of the life cycle—one that Hurst calls "creative destruction"—is necessary.

All too often it is success that breeds complacency. It is hard for organizations, and individuals in them, to not become complacent when they are enjoying success. It is even harder to recognize complacency for what it is. We tend to think what we are doing is right, and what has made us successful will carry us into the future. Instead of complacency, what is needed is a sense of urgency about the renewal of our organization—no matter how well we are presently doing—and the patience to see it through.

The Paradoxes of Leadership

Leaders must have strong positions and be unattached to particular outcomes. This paradox emerged from my refection on the effective leaders I have known, my own engagement in leadership, and on the writing of Angeles Arrien. In the *Four-Fold Way*, Arrien suggests there are important leadership and life lessons we can learn from indigenous people. The first is to use the "power of position." Power of position is not about occupying a role in the organization; instead, it is about having a position on important leadership tasks and management issues. It is, in Arrien's words, "to let others know where we stand, where we don't stand, what we stand for, and how we stand up for ourselves" (1993, p. 24). Having and communicating a stand is being authentic, showing up as true self, and claiming our personal power. It is making the contribution that is distinctively ours to make. Knowing and stating our position builds our personal power and builds trust in relationships.

The seeming paradox that Arrien offers is to "be open to outcome, not attached to outcome." Arrien goes on to define attachments as "specific, immovable expectations, desires that are projected onto people, places, and situations. When we are attached, we often become controlling and rigid" (1993, p. 111). The opposite of attachment is detachment. Arrien says, "When we use the word detachment here, we are speaking of nonattachment, letting go, maintaining our sense of humor. If we observe what causes us to lose our sense of humor, we can identify our point of attachment" (1993, p. 111). Detachment does not mean not caring; it means being flexible rather than rigid and open to outcomes rather than controlling. Understood in this way the paradox could be re-stated as *having a strong position but being detached from a particular outcome.*

Consider the leadership task of creating a vision or a clear sense of direction as an example of the both/and nature of this paradox. It is important for those involved in this task, including the person usually designated as "the leader," to have a position on the preferred future of the organization. Plus it is important that "the leader" state this position clearly and cleanly—no hiding, no fudging, no equivocating, no tentative language, no apologizing. Paradoxically, it is also important to sufficiently detach from the vision to avoid becoming rigid and trying to control the outcome. A vision is not an act of co-creation if any one person forces the outcome. A vision of greatness for an organization emerges from the quality of interaction of key stakeholders. It evolves from the give-and-take of conversations in which every person involved has a position, states that position, and is open to the vision that emerges.

Leaders gain power by giving it away. When you and I do not feel we have enough power we tend to hoard what we have: we withhold information, we tightly control who is involved in accomplishing leadership tasks, we control perks and privileges, and we don't delegate important decisions. The first paradox about power is when we hoard it we lose it.

As I write this I am observing this paradox of hoarding and losing playing out in a large and important local nonprofit educational organization. According to another executive of the organization, the president is a "one-man band." Rather than involve others in making decisions that directly affect them, he makes the decisions by himself. Rather than being open and transparent with important information, he "holds his cards close to his vest."

This president hoards power, and because he does, he has lost power—the staff of the organization no longer grants him any authority. In a very real sense the president has been fired by those who work for him. He still has coercive power he can use in limited areas, but this, I remind you, is not a source of real power.

There was another option for this president, as there is for anyone engaged in leadership: gain power by giving it away. Share information, all of it—the good, the bad, and the ugly. Be transparent; don't keep secrets. Delegate important decisions. Involve others in creating a vision and charting a direction. Trust others to help navigate the difficult white-waters of change. Engage others in defining important core values. Had the president done this, others would have granted him authority. They would have honored his right to exercise the "power of position"—to take strong positions on issues and opportunities, to let them know what he valued and where his boundaries were, and to exert influence.

The option for the president was to believe in abundance rather than scarcity. Power is not a zero sum game. Giving power away does not mean the president would have had less of it. Instead, and paradoxically, the president of this fine educational institution would have gained power by giving it away.

Leaders combine professional will and personal humility. This is a paradox named by Jim Collins in his well-researched and superbly written book, *Good to Great.* Collins wrote, "Compared to high profile leaders with big personalities who make headlines and become celebrities, the good-to-great leaders seem to have come from Mars. Self-effacing, quiet, reserved, even shy—these leaders are a *paradoxical blend* of personal humility and professional will. They are more like Lincoln and Socrates than Patton or Caesar" (2001, p. 13, emphasis added).

Having professional will means that good-to-great leaders have a clear and firm commitment to producing results for the organization, rather than on achieving outcomes for the satisfaction of their egos and the headlines that might result. These men and women are focused and determined, willing to take risks and make tough decisions for the good of the company. They are hard-working and diligent. They use their personal power. They are, as one president said to Collins, "plow horses," not "show horses."

These leaders also have personal humility. They don't seek headlines or the limelight. They don't do things to embellish their own status or prestige. They have ego strength but are not egocentric. They don't call attention to their accomplishments, but instead, when things go well they credit "luck" or other people of the organization.

Earlier I wrote that the very process by which individuals become organizational leaders—the steps up the corporate ladder with an increasing array of perks and privileges at each rung—bend some people out of shape. Strong, healthy egos become supersized. Identity gets warped. Too often what happens to individuals as they climb the organizational ladder stands in contrast with the humility that is needed for effective leadership. Collins says it this way:

> The great irony is that the animus and personal ambition that drive people to positions of power stands at odds with the humility required for Level 5 leadership [by definition, these are leaders who combine professional will and personal humility] When you combine this irony with the fact that boards of directors frequently operate under the false belief that they need to hire a larger-than-life, egocentric leader to make an organization great, you can quickly see why Level 5 leaders rarely appear at the top of our institutions [2001, p. 37].

But it does not have to be this way. There are individuals who climb the organizational ladder and keep their egos in check; their ambition is for the organization not for themselves. There are men and women who ascend to the top of the organizational hierarchy and then turn the hierarchy on its side, executives who understand their role as serving the needs of the organization and the needs of those on the frontline who are ultimately responsible for greatness.

I recently had the opportunity to meet and get to know one of these executives. When I think of Level 5 leadership I think of him. The organization he serves is a leader in its industry, has been ranked by *Fortune* magazine as one of the best places to work in America, and is an organization that consistently produces outstanding results. The president has a clear commitment to the organization and strong ambition for it. He sets a high bar for his performance and for the accomplishment of the organizational mission. But he has little personal ambition. He does not have a reserved parking space. He works in a cubicle like everyone else. He does not call attention to himself—when I heard him speak he told stories of the men and women who made the organization great, and when I watched a film celebrating the company's history I became aware that the story focused on the contributions of employees in the field.

This president was at the top of his organizational hierarchy, but this is not the only place, or even the usual place, to find Level 5 leadership. Level 5 leadership can and does happen throughout an organization or community.

You and I can learn to embrace the paradox of professional will and personal humility and engage in Level 5 leadership, but there are no tips and techniques or comfortable formulas that will get us there. What we do matters less than who we are. Effective leadership, Level 5 leadership, is rooted in our identity. If you want to engage in Level 5 leadership, don't become a leader, become yourself. Your true self. Your authentic self. And this, I remind you, is about inner development as much as it is about outer work.

Paradoxes of the Journey to True Self

It is when I lose myself that I find myself. I have read and heard this idea expressed in many ways and at different times in my faith tradition. The saying "if you want to find your life you must lose it" is repeated six times in one way or another in the first three books of the New Testament. But it is not a saying I quickly or deeply understood, much less appreciated. The meaning was not clear, and, again, I like clarity. And I prize winning much more than losing, whether it was in a Little League baseball game, a game of ping-pong with my younger sister, or getting superb evaluations from clients today. The idea of losing to gain made little or no sense to me.

It has only been in the second half of my life—what Jung called the "afternoon" of life—that I got some sense of how this saying might have meaning. Today I understand this paradox to mean that it is when I let go of my false self and get beyond my egocentric desires that I have the possibility of finding the real self that resides at the center of my being. I must lose false self and ego self to find true self. It is on the other side of pretense and pride that authentic self resides.

This is another paradox that is hard to embrace. As suggested earlier, the false self we have carefully crafted or the ego self that has slowly ballooned can become our fundamental reality. The idea that there is something more—a core self that resides at the center of our being—doesn't compute, at least not in the "morning" of a career and life. But at some point, many of us recognize a gnawing sense within us that there is something more. It often comes with the slow realization that the ladder we have climbed and the life we have lived are not our own, that the person we have become is not who we started out to be. In times like these we understand we must lose ourselves to find ourselves, and when we do, we turn the corner toward home.

I have found that the self that most leaders need to lose if they are to find authentic self is their supersized ego-self. Earlier I wrote that we simply cannot be effective in our leadership role without a strong, healthy ego. But when we confuse ego-self with true self, we lose touch with who we are at the core of our being. When we think that our ego self is our fundamental reality, we lose our way. When meeting the needs and desires of our ego-self becomes more important than serving the needs of the organization, we and the organization suffer.

There is action in non-action. I learned of this paradox and began to grapple with its meaning from two very different sources: the writing of Carl Jung and, surprisingly, a tree. For much of my life I have thought I must make things happen. If I were going to learn and grow and change, become my true authentic self, it would be through the force of my will, because I was proactive, and because of decisions I made and the determination I had. I worked hard to develop my strengths and eliminate or at least disguise my weaknesses. Then I read a book by Carl Jung in which he talked about the art of letting things happen, and he suggested that there is action in non-action. I understood this intellectually, but it was an on-the-top-of-the-surface understanding. I didn't understand it deeply enough to change my beliefs or my behaviors; I kept trying to manufacture my own formation and development.

Some time later I was on a retreat and was invited to have a live encounter with a tree and ask the tree what it could tell me about the winter paradox of dormancy and deep growth. The very idea of having a live encounter with a tree took me by surprise, but I was even more surprised with what the tree had to say to me: "your roots cannot sink deeply into the soil that sustains you unless you have time for dormancy. And a fifteen-minute nap after lunch is not enough. There is action in non-action." I was ready for this lesson; all my busyness and action, my sense than I always had to be doing something useful and the realization that identity was tied to being useful, had left me drained and tired. I was living life on the surface, moving at something approaching warp speed from one assignment to another. I had forgotten the rhythm of activity and rest.

So much for speed, I thought after my visit with the tree, and for being on 24/7. So much for thinking everything depends on my making things happen. And so much for believing that doing something—doing anything—is always better than doing nothing.

To be sure, doing something is sometimes important; there are times when we must be intentional and proactive about our development or formation. There is feedback we ask for and receive, workshops or academic courses to attend, spiritual directors to learn with and from, books to read, and life experiences from which we can and must learn. We are not simply passive recipients; there are things we can and must do to foster our formation. But the paradox of *action in non-action* reminds us that some of our growth and change happens organically and when we appear dormant. It happens from naturally occurring events, not only from things we have planned or made happen.

There are also times when we must be proactive in accomplishing leadership tasks. We can invite all stakeholders to engage in a conversation about the direction of the organization or civic group. We can state our position on key issues, or speak our truth rather than remaining silent when the heat is on. We can put our shoulder to the flywheel and push forward. But there are times, we learn, to leave things alone, to do nothing—we allow an idea about a new direction to simmer on a back burner, we hold our tongue rather than try to fix a broken relationship, we decide not to decide. In these times there is action in non-action.

The more of my darkness (my shadow) I embrace, the more light I dis-

cover. I told the story in chapter two of my journey in and down to name, embrace, and begin the process of integrating my shadow. I didn't want to go there. I was afraid of the dark. I resisted, using every possible defense mechanism known to humankind. But the therapist with whom I was working was as tough as she was tender, and she would not let me off the hook. She turned out to be a great guide for this leg of my journey—she allowed me to travel at my own speed, did not rush the process, allowed me to stop and start and, at times, to turn back. But she also kept nudging, asking me first to name the "monsters" that dwelled inside me, then to greet them as I would a stranger at my front door, then to embrace them as I would a dance partner, and finally to integrate them. You will remember my hope was to get rid of the monsters that created so much havoc in my life, so getting to the point of integrating them was a piece of work. Somewhere along the way I realized I could not be whole—could not be "perfectly Russ"—without doing this hard work of integration. And at some point on the journey I understood and named the paradox: the more darkness I discovered the more light I found. Amazing!

Becoming an authentic and trustworthy leader requires that we embrace this paradox. From my perspective, it is the hardest part of the journey to becoming a whole and authentic person and leader. We act in our leadership roles as though we cast only light, never shadow. This is pretense, an illusion that does not serve us well. Leaders not only cast shadow, the shadow cast is toxic, not benign. Because of their position and power and place in the hierarchy, leaders cast a longer shadow than others. Until leaders acknowledge they have a shadow and begin the hard work of integrating it, they will continue to create shadowy places where others must work.

Even when we acknowledge that we have a shadow, we like to think we can keep it hidden in the substrate of our life, and that we can control it, but this is also not true, at least not true over the long haul. As suggested earlier, our shadow will pop out to haunt us and hurt others, and it usually makes its appearance at all the wrong times. Until we integrate our shadow, fuse it into our identity, we will continue to project it onto those with whom we work. But when we have the courage to take the journey down and in to meet and then embrace our shadow, we will discover light.

Literally and metaphorically, the way to get through winter is to get into it. I lived in Alaska for two years. The winters were hard on me, the dark as much as the cold. In the middle of winter I found myself staying inside, not being very physically active, and sleeping much more than usual. I didn't have much energy. One day a therapist, a woman who worked for the Cabin Fever Clinic in Anchorage—that was the actual name of her organization—made a presentation at my company's "brown bag" luncheon series. Among other things, she told us the best way to get through winter was to get into it. I had been doing just the opposite, and, honestly, what she said seemed contradictory. How, I wondered, can you get through something by getting into it? It was too paradoxical for me to embrace on the spot.

But I also knew what I was doing wasn't working. Trying to cope with winter by sleeping through it made me more lethargic and made the winter seem longer. Pretending that the cold didn't have a bite, that getting stuck in a whiteout wasn't scary, and that the dark wasn't all that bad, did not renew or restore me. Hibernation was not a good coping strategy.

What I slowly learned is that whether the winter is in the external world or in my internal one, the therapist was right: I can get through winter by getting into it. When I turn and face into winter, alone or with trustworthy traveling companions, not only I am able to "winter through," but I also learn that the winters of my life have distinct gifts to offer—the gift of seeing myself and others more clearly, the gift of seeing the landscape of my life without the underbrush hiding anything, and the reminder that dormancy is a necessary part of the journey. Being bitterly cold or finding my way through the dark isn't a picnic in the park, but paradoxically, I have learned that getting into winter can be exhilarating and energizing.

This is another paradox that those engaged in leadership must embrace. The first task of leadership, you will remember, is creating a sense of direction. Getting caught in the organizational equivalent of a whiteout, not knowing which way to go, not being able to see what is directly ahead is a hard tough challenge. When the organizational climate is bitterly cold, the tendency is to protect our self with heavy garb and stay in our office. When there is more darkness than light in the organization, when business and morale are low, and layoffs and stress are up, it is easy to hunker down and try to sleep through it.

This is just what the executive director of a nonprofit organization

173

recently tried to do in my area. When things were going well, he was visible, out and about. He was not always open and transparent in his practice of leadership, but he was warm, charming, engaging, and available on a personal level. But when the economy turned south, and the institution's finances with it, the executive director hunkered down, spent much more time in his office, and relied on key allies on the board to help him weather the storm. He did not face into the winter crises and openly acknowledge its bite; instead, he tried to get through it by staying out of it and pretending it did not exist. It did not work for him; it will not work for any of us.

The paradox is true in leadership as in life: the way to get through the cold and dark is to get into it.

The more I acknowledge my limits the stronger I become. The two injunctions from my parents most deeply ingrained in me are to "be perfect" and to "please others." I have worked hard to comply with both. One way I have tried to be perfect was to present to others an idealized picture of myself: I hid or tried to cover up weaknesses, I did not own my biases or prejudices, I hid my shadow. I tried to baffle when I could not dazzle. Not a healthy way to live, not for me and not for those with whom I was in relationship. And I did my dead-level best to please others, especially authority figures in my life. I did not intentionally lie, but I did not always freely share all the data. Too much of the time I told bosses what I thought they wanted to hear. I said "yes" when the right answer was "no."

It has been a long slow process for me to embrace the paradox that the more I acknowledge my limits, the stronger I become. I am learning that when I acknowledge there are things I do not know, answers I do not have and prejudices I do, things I cannot or should not do no matter how important they are, and tasks that are beyond my ability, others see me as stronger, not weaker. I am granted more authority, not less. Just as important, I experience myself as stronger; I discern the ways I have personal power, claim it, and use it.

I am also freer. Leading with the pretense that I know all, can do all, and can be all is leading with a false self. Trying to be this false self may satisfy my ego, at least temporarily, but it disguises my true self. It binds me and keeps me tied in knots. Taking off masks frees me to be who I am, a distinctive combination of gifts and limits. When I do this, I hold myself more lightly, and relationships are easier and healthier.

9. Embracing Paradoxes

It is important that all of us engaged in leadership embrace this paradox. I have known and worked with leaders who thought they must be all and do all; they expected it of themselves and thought others expected it of them. They did not know how to say, "I don't know." They seemed incapable of saying, "I have no idea how to do that." They did not acknowledge their limits, own their weaknesses, or ever admit to self-doubt. They had not learned to "abandon themselves to the strengths of others," to borrow again a phrase from Max DePree (1989). In their attempt to be strong, they appeared weak.

I have known other men and women who were able to acknowledge their limits and, paradoxically, were perceived of as stronger because of it. One story: ten years ago a pastor I know accepted an offer to head a much larger church. It was a scope and scale change for him—a much larger organization with many more staff and a much larger budget. Early in our relationship he said to me, "I have no idea how to lead a church this size. It scares me to death." He also said this to the staff and to other organizational stakeholders. But then he added, "But I am sure we can figure it out together." And they have. Today the organization is healthy and thriving. Staff were and are encouraged to offer their "gifts and skills and energies" to the accomplishment of leadership tasks. The senior pastor is seen as strong, is granted authority by those he serves, and one reason this is so is because he is honest about his gifts and his limits.

I become myself by being part of community. This paradox is difficult for many people, especially those of us living in the United States, to understand, much less embrace. We confuse individuation with rugged individualism. We believe completing the process of becoming a distinct and whole individual means we must stand on our own two feet, make tough decisions by ourselves, and always be independent. We still love the Lone Ranger, literally and symbolically. Any sign of being dependent on others is seen a weakness; being part of community and acting inter-dependently are seen as soft. Organizations reinforce this. Though companies say they want cross-functional cooperation and good teamwork, by and large it is individual performance that gets rewarded. We fear we cannot be our self and still be part of community. As a result our process of individuation—of becoming our true self—suffers, as does our experience of community.

Some organizations, however, and the people in them are embracing this paradox. TDIndustries is one such company. TDI is a mechanical contracting and service company located in Texas. It works in the world of commercial and residential construction. It is the kind of company where you might reasonably expect to find a lot of rugged individualists and nothing that approached "soft" leadership. But in fact, TDI helps individual employees fulfill their individual potential and become the best they are capable of being. One way it does this is by helping them experience the company as family. Family is a metaphor used often in the company. In a conference I attended, I heard Jack Lowe, Jr., son of the founder, say something like, "It is family. But it is more like brothers and sisters, not parents and children." The need to fulfill individual potential and the need for family create and deepen each other. It is not either/or; it is both/and.

People in Zimbabwe have a Shona word, *ubuntu,* which is difficult to translate into English. In essence it means that my humanity is interdependent with your humanity. It says I am a person because I belong. The same is true for all of us. The solitary human being is a contradiction in terms. It is a contradiction, but it is how those of us in the West have been taught to think.

This does not mean we do not need solitude, or we don't need to become distinct persons capable of standing on our own two feet. It does mean our need for individuation and our need for community enhance and nurture each other. And it means we cannot have one without the other.

To become fully myself, to travel to the center of my being and find true self, I need the experience of live encounters and authentic relationships. I cannot become my self by myself. But my soul—my essence—knows the difference between relationships that are authentic and those that are contrived. Authentic relationships welcome my soul so it shows up; contrived communities and artificial relationships send it into hiding so I show up wearing one mask and then another. The family feeling of TDIndustries was not engineered or manufactured; there was no lever to pull to create the experience of real community. It grew slowly and organically, and grew as all the men and women of the organization learned to relate out of a deep sense of identity and integrity.

9. Embracing Paradoxes

The more I care for and accept myself the more I can care for and accept others. Growing up I learned to think there was a dualism of self versus others. I learned this from parents, from teachers, and from aunts and uncles. There was a right side of the dualism on which to focus: others. Doing this was a mark of maturity. Taking care of self was equated with being selfish.

A clergy friend believes this so deeply that she spends her personal and professional life "emptying herself" or "pouring herself out" for others. She thinks this is what is asked of her, what she agreed to do when she answered the call to be a clergy person. She is often exhausted—physically, mentally, emotionally, even spiritually. She is spent, running on empty much of the time.

What I have learned over time is that there is a difference in self-care and being selfish. Self-care is not an act of self-aggrandizement. It is not evidence of narcissism. It does not preclude caring for others; it is, rather, essential to doing so. There is no self versus others reality; there is only a both/and paradox.

Self-care is taking care of our self, our true self. It is honoring and honing the gifts that define the distinctive contribution we can make to the accomplishment of leadership tasks. It is stopping long enough in the hectic and fast-paced world to allow our souls to catch up with the rest of us. It is knowing what gives us life and energy and what leaves us drained and dispirited. Self-care is taking time to re-member all those disparate parts of our self so that we can engage in leadership as whole men and women. It is making sure we are able to show up at work with all of our energies—mental, physical, emotional, and spiritual. It is making sure there is congruence between inner life and outer work as we engage in leadership.

When we exercise this kind of self-care, we will be better able to accept and care for those with whom we work, and do it in a way they deserve. The more we honor our gifts the better able we are to honor the gifts of others. The more we show up with all our energies the more we encourage others to do the same. The more clarity we have about our core values, the values that animate us, the less threatened we are when others have values that are different. The list goes on.

As does the journey.

177

A Final Hope

As I was writing this book I reflected on my journey to becoming the person I started out to be. As I suspected, the very act of reflecting and writing helped me make sense out of my journey, provided me new and deeper insights into what it means for me to become and be myself, to show up in leadership roles with all my gifts and skills and energies, and to become and be whole and authentic. My deep hope is that something similar has happened for you as you read it.

Postscript:
Leadership Development
Is Personal Development
Is Spiritual Development

Over the past several years I have been thinking about, working with, and writing about how the threads of leader development, personal development, and spiritual development might be woven. In the preface of this book I said I liked to take what the poet Rainer Maria Rilke said were "ill-matched threads and weave them into a single cloth." When I started considering the interrelationship of these three different aspects of development, the threads seemed ill-matched to me and they may seem ill-matched to you now. You may be saying something like, "never the twain shall meet." If so, you are not alone.

I started thinking about the connection of leader development and spiritual development years ago when I read an article by Peter Vaill, a friend and gifted writer and teacher, who wrote: "to a large extent, executive development for leadership in organizations is spiritual development" (1998, p. 208). I was persuaded by the arguments in his paper even as I had doubts about how I might ever use them. But I was sufficiently intrigued by his ideas that I invited him to present a colloquium at CCL. He graciously agreed. His presentation attracted a large audience, including many skeptics, and the discussion that followed was lively, informative and at times a bit heated. It was important enough for me that I reread his paper, took his ideas out of my mental file box, and started working with them more seriously. I had played in the shallow water with these ideas, but decided it was time to dive into the deep end.

At about this same time two colleagues at CCL and I decided to cohost a two-day conference at the beginning of each year to explore the connection of spirit and leadership. People came from many different places—literally and metaphorically—but with a common interest: to discuss how they experienced spirit, or the lack of it, in various practices of leadership. There were no papers or panels, no experts or gurus, but there was rich good conversation, deep probing, and real dialogue. I learned a lot from others about the intersection of leadership and spirit in these conferences during the ten years they were held.

Then in the late 1990s I was offered an opportunity by an editor at Jossey-Bass to write a book about a topic that was important to me. This invitation came as a result of another book I coedited and coauthored, *The Center for Creative Leadership Handbook on Leadership Development,* which was also published by Jossey-Bass. I knew I wanted to continue to explore the intersection of leadership and spirit, but I wasn't just in the deep end, I was in over my head. But I wrote, and learned as I wrote, and the book that resulted, *Leadership and Spirit,* was published in 1999.

One of the people that Jossey-Bass asked to review *Leadership and Spirit* before its publication was, fortunately for me, Peter Vaill. At that time Peter served on the Board of Govenors at CCL and he asked if he could give me his feedback about the book over a breakfast meeting while he was in Greensboro for a board meeting. I gladly agreed. Some 15 years later I still remember the conversation. Peter suggested some changes in the structure of the book that were helpful and important, but the most memorable and energizing part of the conversation was about the topic itself. Peter was pleased that I was going beyond "empiricism, rationalism, and scientism"—things that he said too often "hold us captive"—to lay claim to some different truths, truths that can be known only when looking through what Ken Wilber calls the "eyes of contemplation."

Seeing through eyes of contemplation and linking non-scientific truths about leadership and spirit was once hard for me. By personality preferences, I consider something to be true if it is known to one of my senses—if I can see it, touch it, or smell it. I want to make decision based on a logical and rational analysis of data. I am much more a realist than an idealist, always have been, always will be.

At the same time, and from many diverse experiences, I have learned the importance of seeing through the eyes of contemplation. One small example that had a big impact: as I read Joseph Jaworkski's *Synchronicity: The Inner Path of Leadership*, I realized I had experienced things that could not be explained by my rational logical mind. I knew of the idea of synchronicity from the writing of Carl Jung—that it is an experience of a link between our inner psyche and some external event (I think of you and later that day you call)—but until reading Jaworski I had not linked synchronicity and leadership. Reflecting on this book and relating it to my experience was just one of the things that opened my eyes to new possibilities.

Today I know that some of my most important and defining realities are not known to me through my senses, as important as they still are to me: an experience of what Jewish theologian Martin Buber calls an "I-Thou" relationship, the realization that a breath of fresh air has blown into a stale work or marriage relationship, an awareness that something special and different was happening in a group of which I was a member as we tackled a tough issue with honesty and kindness, or the intuitive sense—a sixth sense—that a direction or decision was right even when there was not hard data to prove it.

These experiences brought me back to Peter Vaill's assertion and to the central message of this postscript: properly understood, leader development is personal development is spiritual development. Let's connect the dots.

By now you know that the primary message of this book: *becoming a leader is becoming yourself.* The purpose of leader development is to help us become ourselves, the person we started out to be.

When leader development is understood in this way, leader development and personal development have the same purpose: helping individuals become authentic and integrated human beings. In the introduction to *On Becoming a Leader,* Warren Bennis made the same point:

> My view is based on the assumption that leaders are people who are able to express themselves fully. By this I mean that they know who they are, what their strengths and weaknesses are, and how to fully deploy their

strengths and compensate for their weaknesses ... the key to full self-expression is understanding one's self and the world, and the key to understanding is learning—from one's own life and experiences ... in fact, *the process of becoming a leader is much the same as becoming an integrated human being.* For the leader, as for any integrated person, life itself is the career [1989, pp. 3–4, emphasis added].

The late Carl Rogers said much the same thing. In *On Becoming a Person,* Rogers described becoming ourselves as our "actualizing tendency." He argued that you and I slowly evolve due to "the directional trend which is evident in all organic and human life—the urge to expand, extend, mature—the tendency to express and activate all the capacities of the organization, or the self" (1961, p. 351). Sound familiar? From my perspective Rogers and Bennis are saying the same thing: our growth is toward becoming a person, toward becoming ourselves. If anything Rogers takes it one step further: he calls it a directional trend, one that is evident in nature and human life.

Admittedly, I have offered brief sketches of complex theories, but the important assumption underlying each of them is that we do grow, change, evolve, and that our growth has an "actualizing tendency." I know some people devolve, that the difficult experiences of their lives continue to bend them more and more out of their original shape. But for most of us the "actualizing tendency" takes us in the direction of becoming ourselves. This evolution to true self is neither quick nor easy. We are always in the process of being and becoming. The journey continues our whole life. Some of us are unwilling to take the journey; others start it but turn back before it is complete. But those of us who stay the course can become the person we started out to be, at least we become that person in single hours or single experiences. We find our own truth, our own voice, move toward wholeness or integration, and are authentic in leadership and life. One more time: properly understood, leader development and personal development share the same basic purpose.

There is one more thread—one more seemingly "ill-suited thread"—to add to this cloth we are weaving. It may appear the most ill-suited of all and especially ill-suited by those who are held captive by empiricism and rationalism. That thread is the thread of spiritual development. It is time to weave it into the same cloth as leader development and personal development. We have woven the threads of leader and personal development by describing how a key purpose of both is to help us become integrated people, fully and wholly who we are. But what about spiritual development, what is the purpose of it and how can it be woven into this cloth?

One of my favorite religious writers is the late Trappist monk, Thomas Merton. In *New Seeds of Contemplation,* Merton says we must move beyond ego self and false self, the self we carefully craft to satisfy the expectations of others, if we are to find true self. This is one of the best ways I know to describe the purpose of the spiritual journey: to find true self, the self that exists on the other side of our egocentric desires, the self that resides at the center of our being. Merton adds:

> There is in us an instinct for newness, for renewal, for liberation of creative power ... and yet this same instinct tells us that this change is a recovery of what is deepest, most original, most personal in ourselves. To be born again is not to become somebody else, *but to become ourselves ... the deepest spiritual instinct in man is the inner truth which demands that he be faithful to himself, to his deepest and most original potentialities ... to become one's true self, the false self must die* [2002, p. 64, emphasis added].

I started the second chapter with a quote from Warren Bennis which said, in part, "The point is not to become a leader. The point is to become yourself ... the person you started out to be." Merton is saying that the spiritual journey has the same purpose: to become ourselves and be faithful to ourselves.

Merton goes on to suggest what I have said earlier in this book, the journey to becoming ourselves is a long, hard journey. The reason this is so is that we begin to think our false self is the fundamental reality of our life. Merton writes, "Every one of us is shadowed by an illusory person, a false self ... this is the man I want to be but who cannot exist ... all sin [dividedness, brokenness] starts from the assumption that this false self is the fundamental reality of life to which everything else in the universe is ordered" (2002, pp. 56, 57). Because we think of our false self as our real self it takes many years—and some failings and fallings and hardships—for us to turn toward home, toward true self. But this is the purpose of leader development, personal development and spiritual development. We use different language to describe all three, but the language used points us to the same reality: the point is to become our self, our true self, and to become a whole and authentic person and leader.

Much more could be said, and deserves to be said, about leader development and personal development and spiritual development. Dig more deeply into any one of the three and differences will emerge. I do not care to minimize the differences. But for me the essential purpose of all three is the same. Peter Vaill was right: *properly understood, leader development is personal development is spiritual development.*

Leader development and personal development and spiritual development are not three dots that can be connected. They are the same dot seen from different perspectives.

This postscript was written for those who are interested in exploring one more way to see things whole. As I have said, I learn while I write, and writing about these ideas is one way I learn about their interrelationships. I invite you to help in this exploration by sharing your ideas and perspectives. You can send your responses or ideas to me at rmoxley93@gmail.com.

References

Arrien, A. 1993. *The Four-Fold Way.* San Francisco: Harper San Francisco.

Barron, R. January 2, 2011. "Center Has Nurtured Leaders for 40 Years." *The News and Record.* Greensboro, NC.

Bennis, W. August 18, 1997. "Cultivating Creative Genius." *Industry Week.* p. 84.

Bennis, W. 1989. *On Becoming a Leader.* Reading, MA: Addison-Wesley.

Bennis, W., and P.W. Biederman. 1997. *Organizing Genius: The Secrets of Creative Collaboration.* Reading, MA: Addison-Wesley.

Bennis, W., and R. Thomas. September 2002. "Crucibles of Leadership." *Harvard Business Review.*

Berry, W. 2000. *Jayber Crow.* Washington, D.C.: Counterpoint.

Block, P. 2002. *The Answer to How Is Yes: Acting on What Matters.* San Francisco: Berrett-Koehler Publishers.

Block, P. 2008. *Community: The Structure of Belonging.* San Francisco: Berrett-Koehler Publishers.

Block, P. 1993. *Stewardship: Choosing Service Over Self-Interest.* San Francisco: Berrett-Koehler Publishers.

Buber, M. 1970. *I and Thou.* New York: Scribner.

Bunker, K., and M. Wakefield. 2005. *Leading with Authenticity in Times of Transition.* Greensboro, NC: The Center for Creative Leadership.

Collins, J. 2001. *Good to Great.* New York: HarperCollins.

DePree, M. 1989. *Leadership Is an Art.* New York: Doubleday.

Ernst, Chris, and D. Chrobot-Mason. 2010. *Boundary Spanning Leadership: Six Practices for Solving Problems, Driving Innovation, and Transformating Organizations.* New York: McGraw-Hill.

Freiberg, K., and J. Freiberg. 1996. *Nuts!* Austin, TX: Bard Press.

George, B., P. Sims, A. McLean, and D. Meyer. February 2007. "Discovering Your Authentic Leadership." *Harvard Business Review.*

Goffee, R., and G. Jones. December 2005. "Managing Authenticity: The Paradox of Great Leadership." *Harvard Business Review.*

Gordon, T. 1977. *Leader Effectiveness Training.* New York: G.P. Putnam's Sons.

Handy, C. 1994. *The Age of Paradox.* Boston: Harvard Business School Press.

Handy, C. 1998. *The Hungry Spirit.* New York: Broadway Books.

References

Harnish, J. 2004. *You Only Have to Die: Leading Your Congregation to New Life.* Nashville, TN: Abingdon Press.

Harvey, J. 1998. *The Abilene Paradox and Other Meditations on Management.* Lexington, MA: Heath.

Heenan, D., and W. Bennis. 1999. *Co-Leaders: The Power of Great Partnerships.* New York: John Wiley & Sons.

Heifetz, R. 1994. *Leadership Without Easy Answers.* Cambridge, MA: Harvard University Press.

Heifetz, R., and M. Linsky. 2002. *Leadership on the Line.* Boston: Harvard Business School Press.

Hock, D. 1999. *Birth of the Chaordic Age.* San Francisco: Berrett-Koehler.

Hurst, D., and B. Zimmerman. 2002. *Crises and Renewal: Meeting the Challenge of Organizational Change.* Boston: Harvard Business School Press.

Jacobi, J. 1973 [1942]. *The Psychology of C.J. Jung.* New Haven, CT: Yale University Press.

Jaworski, J. 1996. *Synchronicity: The Inner Path of Leadership.* San Francisco: Berrett-Koehler.

Jobs, Steve. September 2, 2005. "Stay Hungry. Stay Foolish." *Fortune.*

Jung, C.G. 1993 [1959]. *The Basic Writings of C.J. Jung.* S. de Laszlo, ed. New York: Modern Library.

Jung, C.G. 1960. *The Collected Writings of C.G. Jung.* Translated by Gerhard Adler and R.F.C. Hull. Princeton, NJ: Princeton University Press.

Kegan, R. 1982. *The Evolving Self.* Cambridge, MA: Harvard University Press.

Kidd, S.M. 1990. *When the Heart Waits.* New York: HarperCollins.

Koestenbaum, Peter. 1991. *Leadership: The Inner Side of Greatness.* San Francisco: Jossey-Bass.

Kotter, J. 1990. *A Force for Change: How Leadership Differs from Management.* New York: Free Press.

Kotter, J. 2008. *A Sense of Urgency.* Boston: Harvard Business School Press.

Leonard, G. 1978. *The Silent Pulse.* New York: Dutton.

MacKenzie, Gordon. 1996. *Orbiting the Giant Hairball: A Corporate Fool's Guide to Surviving with Grace.* New York: Penguin Group.

McCall, M. 1998. *High Flyers: Developing the Next Generation of Leaders.* Boston: Harvard Business School Press.

McCall, M., and G. Hollenbeck. Eds. K. Bunker, D. Hall and K. Kram. 2010. "The Not-So-Secret Sauce of the Leadership Development Recipe." In *Extraordinary Leadership: Addressing the Gap in Senior Executive Development.* San Francisco: Jossey-Bass.

McCauley, C., and E. Van Velsor. 2004. *The Center for Creative Leadership Handbook on Leadership Development.* San Francisco: Jossey-Bass.

McGuire, John B., Chuck S. Palus, William Passmore and Gary Rhodes. 2009. *Transforming Your Organization.* Greensboro, NC: Center for Creative Leadership.

Merton, T. 1961. *New Seeds of Contemplation.* New York: New Directions.

Merton, T. 2002. *Essential Writings.* C. Bochen, ed. Maryknoll, NY: Orbis Books.

Moore, Thomas. 2001. *Original Self.* New York: HarperCollins.

Moxley, R. 2000. *Leadership and Spirit.* San Francisco: Jossey-Bass.

Moxley, R., and M. L. Pulley. 2004.

References

"Hardships." *The Center for Creative Leadership Handbook of Leadership Development*, eds. Cindy McCauley and Ellen Van Velsor. San Francisco: Jossey-Bass.

Muller, W. 1999. *Sabbath: Restoring the Sacred Rhythm of Rest.* New York: Bantam Books.

Nepo, Mark. 2005. *The Exquisite Risk: Daring to Live an Authentic Life.* New York: Harmony Books.

O'Toole, J. 1995. *Leading Change: Overcoming the Ideology of Comfort and the Tyranny of Change.* San Francisco: Jossey-Bass.

Palmer, P. 1990. *The Active Life: Wisdom for Work, Creativity and Caring.* New York: HarperCollins.

Palmer, P. 2004. *A Hidden Wholeness: The Journey to an Undivided Life.* San Francisco: Jossey-Bass.

Palmer, P. 2000. *Let Your Life Speak.* San Francisco: Jossey-Bass.

Parker, Michael. 2014. *All I Have in This World.* Chapel Hill, NC: Algonquin Books.

Peters, Thomas J., and Robert H. Waterman, Jr. 1982. *In Search of Excellence: Lessons from America's Best-Run Companies.* New York: Harper and Row.

Robinson, M. 2004. *Gilead.* New York: Farrar, Strauss and Giroux.

Rogers, C. 1961. *On Becoming a Person.* Cambridge, MA: Riverside Press.

Rohr, Richard. 2011. *Falling Upward:* *A Spirituality for the Two Halves of Life.* San Francisco: Jossey-Bass.

Sarton, May. 1993. "Now I Become Myself." *Collected Poems, 1930–1993.* New York: W. W. Norton and Company.

Satir, Virginia. 1972. *Peoplemaking.* Palo Alton, CA: Science and Behavior Books.

Vaill, Peter B. 1998. *Spirited Leading and Learning: Process Wisdom for a New Age.* San Francisco: Jossey-Bass.

Walsh, D.C. 2006. *Trustworthy Leadership: Can We Become the Leaders We Want Our Students to Be?* Hoboken, NJ: John Wiley and Sons.

Waterman, R. 1987. *The Renewal Factor.* New York: Bantam Books.

Wheatley, M. 2005. *Finding Our Way: Leadership for an Uncertain Time.* San Francisco: Berrett-Koehler.

Wheatley, M. 1992. *Leadership and the New Science.* San Francisco: Berrett-Koehler.

Whyte, D. 1994. *The Heart Aroused: Poetry and the Preservation of the Soul in Corporate America.* New York: Doubleday.

Wilson, L. 1987. *Changing the Game: The New Way to Sell.* New York: Simon & Schuster.

Wolcott, Derek. 1986. *Collected Poems, 1948–1984.* New York: Farrar, Straus & Giroux.

Index

189

Index

Index